Second Edition

Listen To Me!

Beginning Listening, Speaking & Pronunciation

Barbara H. Foley

**Institute for Intensive English
Union County College, New Jersey**

Heinle & Heinle Publishers
A Division of Wadsworth, Inc.
Boston, MA 02116

The publication of *Listen to Me!, Beginning Listening, Speaking, and Pronunciation, Second Edition,* was directed by the members of the Newbury House Publishing Team at Heinle & Heinle:

Erik Gundersen, Editorial Director
Susan Mraz, Marketing Director
Gabrielle B. McDonald, Production Editor

Also participating in the publication of this program were:

Publisher: Stanley J. Galek
Editorial Production Manager: Elizabeth Holthaus
Project Manager: Anita L. Raducanu/A+ Publishing Services
Associate Editor: Lynne Telson Barsky
Assistant Editor: Karen Hazar
Associate Marketing Manager: Donna Hamilton
Production Assistant: Maryellen Eschmann
Manufacturing Coordinator: Mary Beth Lynch
Illustrator: Marcy Ramsey: all illustrations, *except*
          Nathan C. Reilly: pp. 29, 42, 72
Interior Design: Sue Gerould/Perspectives
Composition: A+ Publishing Services
Cover Design: Petra Hausberger

Heinle & Heinle Publishers is a division of Wadsworth, Inc.

Manufactured in the United States of America

Library of Congress Cataloging in Publication Data

Foley, Barbara H.
     Listen to me! : beginning listening comprehension / Barbara H. Foley.
        p.   cm.
     ISBN 0-8384-5264-7
     1. English language--Textbooks for foreign speakers.
  2. Listening.   I. Title.
  PE1128.F567 1993
  428.3'4--dc20   93-25538
                                                          CIP

ISBN: 0-8384-5264-7

10 9 8 7 6

CONTENTS

TO THE TEACHER

English as a second language learners are surrounded by sounds—conversations, announcements, music, television, radio, instructions. Listening is their primary source of language input. Our challenge as teachers is to help students make sense of this incoming stream of language. As learners, our students need practice and listening strategies. As individuals, they need confidence in their ability to understand their new language.

Listen to Me! is a listening text for beginning students of ESL. It develops listening skills for high interest narratives and informal conversations. The text and accompanying tapes may be used with college-level students, adult programs, and high school classes. Additionally, the materials are both easy to use and highly effective in a language laboratory.

Listen to Me! is one in a series of three titles designed to develop aural/oral communication skills. The complete series has been designed to meet the needs of students from the beginning to intermediate levels and includes the following:

- *Listen to Me!*   beginning
- *Now Hear This!*   high beginning
- *That Sounds Good!*   intermediate

There are fifteen units in *Listen to Me!* Each is based on a particular character's job, interests, daily activities, or problems. The units are composed of five sections. In COMPREHENSION, students listen to a one-to-two minute narrative about a character. Through the use of pictures, the narrative is linked to the real situation. Students can follow the visuals, listening to the sound and flow of English. They hear the organization of the language and the sequence and relationships of ideas. Then, through a variety of interactive exercises, they learn to listen for general and specific details. In both the STRUCTURE and PRONUNCIATION sections, students concentrate on language discrimination, listening for structure or phonological features such as reductions, elisions, and intonation. The CONVERSATION section presents three to six short conversations, interview comments, or announcements related to the topic. The interviews and announcements are transcriptions of authentic language. The conversations were roleplayed and scripted, with liberal use of expressions and replies that were recorded while gathering natural speech for this text. Students focus on general meaning and listening strategies. The final section, INTERACTION, gives students the opportunity to share their own interests and opinions in a small group setting. The units follow the format outlined below.

COMPREHENSION

The first part of the unit presents a recorded story, focusing on a particular person's job, family, interests, or problems. The stories are approximately one to two minutes in length. The exercises in this section provide background and vocabulary for the story, help students follow the story line, and ask students to listen for specific information.

Discuss

The questions in this section introduce the topic to the class, stimulating students' interest in the selection. Teachers should encourage students to offer information, personal stories, and opinions.

Before You Listen

The short activity in this section builds more specific background for the unit. Students may be asked to identify states, match occupations, make predictions, answer questions about their families, etc.

Key Words

The class looks at the key words and ask about those they do not understand. Before listening to the sentences on the cassette, the teacher might say the vocabulary words and ask students to repeat them. Then, students listen to the sentences on the cassette and write the correct word.

First Listening

The second page of the unit is a full-page illustration that clearly depicts the story, either as one picture or as a series of small sketches. Encourage students to carefully look at the picture, noting actions, relationships, and sequence of events. Students then listen to the recorded story while following the illustrations. Most classes will request that the tape be played again, one or more times. For some classes, it may be helpful to play the tape in sections, a few sentences at a time. After listening, students tell the class any information they remember about the story. The focus here is not on structure, but on the comprehension of the story. One student may only be able to give back one small piece of information. Another may be able to remember many facts. The teacher should prompt students to recall much of the information, especially those parts that are pictured. Students who may have had difficulty understanding the selection will learn from their classmates.

Listen and Write the Letter (or Listen for Numbers)

This activity asks students to identify specific story pictures. While looking at the illustrations, students hear statements from the story. They decide which picture the statement is describing. Occasionally, they must answer questions with a correct number or amount from the story and pictures.

Listen for Specific Information

Depending on the story, students are asked for specific information. They may identify the jobs of the characters, check the items a person bought in a store, choose the doctor's orders, etc.

Comprehension Questions

In the final activity of this section, students hear seven questions about the story and circle the correct answer.

UNIT ORGANIZATION

Structure

In the first part of each unit, the emphasis is on content. In the next two sections, the emphasis shifts to listening discrimination. In the first exercise in STRUCTURE, students focus on verb tense. Although there is a variety of tenses within each selection, one tense usually predominates. Students listen to individual sentences from the listening passage and write the complete verb.

There may be a second structure exercise, directing students to listen for features such as tense contrast, articles, or negatives.

Pronunciation

Within each listening selection, there is often a recurring pronunciation feature. The pronunciation exercises help students to hear word endings, reductions, elisions, intonation, and stress. Students circle the phonological item they hear, complete sentences with the correct word, or mark stress or intonation.

Conversations

This section begins with three to six short conversations, interview comments, or announcements related to the topic. The conversations are purposely pitched at a more difficult level than the narratives, so that students begin to realize that they do not need to understand every word in a conversation. In the first exercise, students guess the general meaning of the conversation by circling a picture identified in the listening passage. Often, simply by recognizing a few of the vocabulary words or phrases in the exchange, students will be able to make their selections. Further exercises develop listening strategies, helping students to become familiar with common conversation techniques, such as continuing the conversation, checking or repeating information, expressing agreement, disagreement, surprise, etc.

Interaction

The INTERACTION is a follow-up speaking activity that allows students to share personal information, ideas and opinions. For the interviews, students sit with a partner. For most other activities, students sit in small groups. The groups should consist of three to four students so that every student has an opportunity to participate.

COMPONENTS

Listen to Me! is a complete and fully-integrated program for students and teachers alike. Complementing the student text is a series of audio cassettes containing all of the listening passages and follow-up activities. A sample cassette may be obtained free of charge from the publisher.

ACKNOWLEDGMENTS

In the revised edition of *Listen to Me!*, I was working from a treasure chest. The original text has been used by thousands of students over the past nine years. By listening carefully, I have been able to apply student and teacher feedback plus new research in the ESL field to add, delete, and change features of the existing program. With much appreciation to the individuals below, the revised edition of *Listen to Me!* is hopefully up-to-date, effective and enjoyable to use.

Thank you to my colleagues at Union County College. You've always been available to share ideas, test materials, and speak into a tape recorder. Special thanks to Howard Pomann, Dorothy Burak, Marinna Kolaitis, Liz Neblett, Larry Wollman, John McDermott, Litza Georgiou, and Andre DeSandies. I am especially grateful for the support of Union County College in granting me a sabbatical in which to complete this project.

The professional staff at Heinle & Heinle compiled program feedback, arranged sharing sessions, and were enthusiastic and supportive throughout the revision of *Listen to Me!* I appreciate the special assistance of Erik Gundersen, Lynne Telson Barsky, Karen Hazar, and Anita Raducanu.

When writing, an author owes a special debt to researchers and theoreticians in the ESL field. Over the past several years, I have read journal articles and books on listening by the following individuals. Additionally, I was privileged to hear all of them speak at International TESOL conferences: Patricia Dunkel, Stephen Krashen, Joan Morley, Pat Wilcox Peterson, Jack Richards, and Penny Ur.

Finally, thank you, Bill, for your constant support and confidence in me.

ALI

COMPREHENSION

A. Discuss

Talk about these questions.

Do you live in a house or in an apartment?
Do you know your neighbors?
Do you talk with them a lot?
What countries are they from?

B. Before You Listen

Match these jobs with the correct picture.

1. _____ x-ray technician

2. _____ letter carrier

3. _____ student

4. _____ telephone operator

5. _____ teacher

C. Key Words

Ask your teacher about any new words below. Listen to the sentences and fill in the correct words.

aunt and uncle	single
relatives	retired
couple	twins

1. My sister and I are both 24. We're _____ .
2. I have a lot of _____ in the United States.
3. I visit my _____ about once a month.
4. George is _____ . He isn't married.
5. My father _____ when he was 65 years old.
6. The _____ who lives under us is very friendly.

1

🔲 D. First Listening

Read the names below. Then look at the picture on page 2 and listen to this story about Ali and the people who live in his apartment building. As you listen, write the names of the people on the picture. Tell the class any information you remember about the story.

Ali	**Manuel and Michael**
Mr. Patel	**Cao**
Mr. and Mrs. Ramirez	**Linh**

🔲 E. Listen and Choose

Read the jobs below. Then listen to the story again. Match each person with his or her job.

1. _____ Ali
2. _____ Mr. Ramirez
3. _____ Mrs. Ramirez
4. _____ Mr. Patel
5. _____ Cao
6. _____ Linh

a. a telephone operator
b. a student
c. an x-ray technician
d. a letter carrier
e. a retired teacher
f. a student

🔲 F. Listen for Numbers

Look at the picture and answer these questions with the correct number.

1. _____
2. _____
3. _____
4. _____

5. _____
6. _____
7. _____
8. _____

🔲 G. Comprehension Questions

Listen and circle the correct answer.

1. a. Egypt   b. Oakdale   c. his aunt and uncle
2. a. in Egypt   b. at the university   c. his aunt and uncle
3. a. on the 1st floor b. on the 2nd floor   c. on the 3rd floor
4. a. Yes, he is.   b. He's a letter carrier. c. He's a telephone operator.
5. a. Egypt   b. India   c. next to Ali
6. a. He's retired.   b. Yes, he is.   c. No, he isn't.
7. a. Yes, they are.   b. No, they aren't.   c. at the university

> • am / is / are
> • a

STRUCTURE

🔲 A. Listen and Write

Listen to these sentences. Write the verb you hear: *am*, *is*, or *are*.

1. ____is____   6. _____
2. _____   7. _____
3. _____   8. _____
4. _____   9. _____
5. _____   10. _____

B. Write

Complete these sentences with *am*, *is*, or *are*.

1. I _____ a student at Oakdale University.
2. There _____ four families in this building.
3. Mr. Ramirez _____ a letter carrier.
4. They _____ twins.
5. They _____ ten years old.
6. Mr. Patel _____ old.
7. He _____ a retired teacher.
8. Cao _____ a student at Oakdale University.
9. All the people _____ friendly.
10. They _____ good neighbors.

PRONUNCIATION

🔲 A. The Article *A*

All of these sentences have the article *a*. Listen carefully and put the article in the correct place in the sentence.

Example: He's ^a^ retired teacher.

1. He's letter carrier.
2. Cao is student.
3. There's family living under us.
4. She's telephone operator.
5. I'm student at Oakdale University.

6. We live in small apartment building.

7. She works in hospital.

8. Mr. Patel is single man.

9. He has lot of relatives.

10. Cao and Linh are young couple from Vietnam.

CONVERSATIONS

🔲 A. Match

Listen to these conversations between people in Ali's apartment building. Number the pictures.

🔲 B. Listen and Answer

Listen to each conversation again. Then answer these questions with your class.

1. Are they late for class?
    What are they going to do?

2. Who is Mr. Patel waiting for?
    Why are the boys busy?

3. When is the first soccer game?
    Where do they play soccer?

🔲 C. *How*

Listen to these questions. Circle *How's* or *How're*.

1. How's   How're
2. How's   How're
3. How's   How're
4. How's   How're
5. How's   How're

6. How's   How're
7. How's   How're
8. How's   How're
9. How's   How're
10. How's   How're

D. Hello and Good-bye

Listen to these expressions. Some you can use when you say *Hello*. Some you can use when you say *Good-bye*. Circle *Hello* or *Good-bye*.

1. Hello   Good-bye   6. Hello   Good-bye
2. Hello   Good-bye   7. Hello   Good-bye
3. Hello   Good-bye   8. Hello   Good-bye
4. Hello   Good-bye   9. Hello   Good-bye
5. Hello   Good-bye   10. Hello   Good-bye

INTERACTION

Your house or apartment is in the middle box. Write the names of the people who live next to you. Write a few sentences about them. Where are they from? What do they do? Are they friendly? Share your information with a partner.

Mr. / Mrs. / Ms. _____ lives on my right.

_____

_____

_____

_____

Mr. / Mrs. / Ms. _____ lives on my left.

_____

_____

_____

_____

BACK IN SCHOOL

COMPREHENSION

A. Discuss

Talk about these questions.

> **Is English easy for you?**
> **How is your English . . . good? so-so? not too good?**
> **Where do you speak English?**

B. Before You Listen

Read these statements. Why are you studying English? Check the reasons that you are in school.

_____ 1. I want to find a job.

_____ 2. I want to find a better job.

_____ 3. I want to understand the radio and television.

_____ 4. I want to talk to my neighbors.

_____ 5. I want to go to the store and use English.

_____ 6. I want to talk to my children's teachers.

_____ 7. I want to go to college.

C. Key Words

Ask your teacher about any new words below. Listen to the sentences and fill in the correct words.

nervous	break
each other	homework
cafeteria	second

1. Our coffee _____ is 15 minutes.

2. I feel _____ when I speak English.

3. This is my _____ year in the United States.

4. For _____ , we have to do pages 14 and 15.

5. We talk to _____ before class.

6. I'm going to the _____ for a cup of coffee.

🔲 D. First Listening

Ana is a student at the Dallas Adult School. Look at the picture on page 8 and listen to her story. After you listen, tell the class any information you remember about the story.

🔲 E. Listen for Numbers

Read these questions about the story. Then listen to the story again and answer these questions with the correct number.

1. What's the date?   _____
2. What is the room number?   _____
3. How old is Ana?   _____
4. How many children does she have?   _____
5. How many students are in her class?   _____
6. How many are from Mexico?   _____
7. How many are from Vietnam?   _____
8. How many are from India?   _____
9. How old is the teacher?   _____
10. How many hours is the class?   _____
11. What time does this class begin?   _____
12. What time is the break?   _____

🔲 F. Listen and Choose

Read these statements, then listen again. Check the reasons that Ana is back in school.

_____ 1. She wants to understand her children.
_____ 2. She wants to get a job.
_____ 3. She wants to talk to her children's teachers.
_____ 4. She wants to talk to her husband.
_____ 5. She wants to go to college.
_____ 6. She wants to learn to type.
_____ 7. She wants to talk to her children's friends.

🔲 G. True or False

Listen to these statements. Circle *T* if the statement is true, *F* if the statement is false.

1. T F		6. T F
2. T F		7. T F
3. T F		8. T F
4. T F		9. T F
5. T F		10. T F

> • **there is / there are / they are**
> • *negatives* **is / isn't**

STRUCTURE

A. Listen and Write

Listen to these sentences. Circle the words you hear: *there is*, *there are*, or *they're*.

1. there is   there are   they're   5. there is   there are   they're

2. there is   there are   they're   6. there is   there are   they're

3. there is   there are   they're   7. there is   there are   they're

4. there is   there are   they're   8. there is   there are   they're

B. Read and Write

Complete these sentences with *there is*, *there are*, or *they're*.

1. _____ one student from India.

2. _____ three students from Vietnam.

3. _____ friendly.

4. _____ in school.

5. _____ a lot of homework.

6. _____ ten students in our class.

7. _____ classes for typing.

8. _____ from Mexico.

PRONUNCIATION

A. Listen for Negatives

Listen carefully for *is* or *isn't*. Circle the word you hear.

1. is   isn't   6. is   isn't

2. is   isn't   7. is   isn't

3. is   isn't   8. is   isn't

4. is   isn't   9. is   isn't

5. is   isn't   10. is   isn't

ANNOUNCEMENTS

A. Match

Ms. Lang, the teacher, made several announcements the first week of school. Match each announcement with one of the topics on the right.

1. _____
2. _____
3. _____
4. _____
5. _____
6. _____

a. parking sticker
b. children
c. break time
d. other classes
e. days absent
f. book

B. True or False

Listen to the announcements again. Decide if the statements are true or false. Circle *T* or *F*.

1. T F   You can buy the English book in the main office.
2. T F   The break is at 10:45.
3. T F   You need a sticker to park in the parking lot.
4. T F   If there is a school holiday, your child can sit very quietly in the back of the classroom.
5. T F   You can take both math and typing classes.
6. T F   If you are absent, call the teacher.

C. Excuse Me

The students are asking Ms. Lang to repeat some information. Listen and complete these conversations.

1. MS. LANG: You can buy the book in the main office.
   STUDENT: Excuse me. _____ ?
2. MS. LANG: The book is $20.
   STUDENT: Excuse me. _____ ?
3. MS. LANG: Class begins at 9:00.
   STUDENT: Excuse me. _____ ?
4. MS. LANG: The break is at 10:30.
   STUDENT: Excuse me. _____ ?
5. MS. LANG: The break is 15 minutes.
   STUDENT: Excuse me. _____ ?
6. MS. LANG: You can get the sticker in the main office.
   STUDENT: Excuse me. _____ ?
7. MS. LANG: A parking sticker is $5.00.
   STUDENT: Excuse me. _____ ?

INTERACTION

Sit in a group of students. Answer these questions together about your class.

1. What's the name of your school? _____

2. What's your room number? _____

3. What's your teacher's name? _____

4. How many students are in your class? _____

5. What countries are the students from? How many are from each country?

Country	Number of Students

6. How many days a week do you
    have English class? _____

7. How long is your English class? _____

8. What time does your English class
    begin? _____

9. What time does it end? _____

10. What time is your break? _____

CITY OR COUNTRY

COMPREHENSION

A. Discuss

Talk about these questions.

> **Is there a hospital in your area?**
> **How large is it?**
> **What kind of hospital is it?**

B. Before You Listen

For some of the words below, we think of the city, and for others we think of the country. Write *city* or *country* on each line.

1. museums   _____

2. theaters   _____

3. mountains   _____

4. rivers   _____

5. many restaurants   _____

6. lakes   _____

7. tall buildings   _____

C. Key Words

Ask your teacher about any new words below. Listen to the sentences and fill in the correct words.

general	takes care of
offers	patients
cancer	choose

1. I don't smoke because I don't want to get _____ .

2. When a child is sick, a parent _____ him.

3. Can you help me _____ a good doctor?

4. When my sister graduated from nursing school, she received three job _____ .

5. A 300-bed hospital has room for 300 _____ .

6. A _____ hospital takes care of all kinds of patients—people with heart problems, people with cancer, and people who were in car accidents.

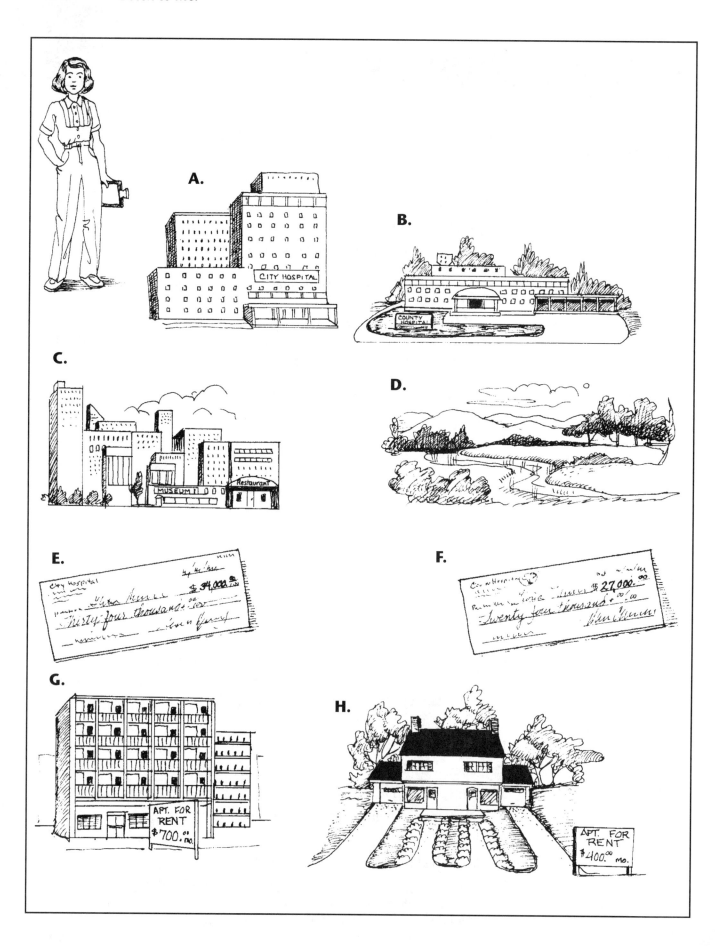

D. First Listening

Gloria is going to graduate from nursing school next month. Look at the pictures on page 14 and listen to the story as many times as you want. After you listen, tell the class any information you remember about the story. How many job offers does Gloria have? Where are they?

E. Listen and Choose

Read each statement. Some are about the hospital in the city; others are about the hospital in the country. Listen to the story again and check *city* or *country* after each sentence.

	city	country
1. It's a 600-bed hospital.	_____	_____
2. It's near the mountains.	_____	_____
3. It takes care of all kinds of patients.	_____	_____
4. The salary is high.	_____	_____
5. It's a general hospital.	_____	_____
6. The salary is average.	_____	_____
7. It's a cancer hospital.	_____	_____
8. It's a 50-bed hospital.	_____	_____

F. Listen and Write the Letter

Listen to these sentences. Write in the letter of the correct picture.

1. _____   5. _____
2. _____   6. _____
3. _____   7. _____
4. _____   8. _____

G. Comprehension Questions

Listen and circle the correct answer.

1. a. a student   b. a nurse   c. Yes, she is.
2. a. She's in the hospital.   b. Yes, she is.   c. No, she isn't.
3. a. It has 50 beds.   b. It has 600 beds.   c. It's a cancer hospital.
4. a. It's large.   b. In the country.   c. In the city.
5. a. a large hospital   b. a cancer hospital c. a general hospital
6. a. $27,000 a year   b. $30,000 a year   c. $34,000 a year
7. a. The one in the country. b. The one in the city. c. She doesn't know.

> • **is / are**
> • *singular or plural*

STRUCTURE

🔲 A. Listen and Write

Listen to these sentences about the story. Write the verb you hear: *is* or *are*.

1. ___is___   6. _____

2. _____   7. _____

3. _____   8. _____

4. _____   9. _____

5. _____   10. _____

PRONUNCIATION

🔲 A. Singular or Plural

Listen to these sentences. Decide if the noun is singular or plural. Circle the word you hear.

1. a. student   b. students
2. a. offer   b. offers
3. a. hospital   b. hospitals
4. a. patient   b. patients
5. a. museum   b. museums
6. a. country   b. countries
7. a. lake   b. lakes
8. a. salary   b. salaries
9. a. rent   b. rents
10. a. hospital   b. hospitals

B. Fill in

Complete these sentences.

1. It's a big hospital, near _____ . (restaurant, restaurants)
2. It's a 600-bed _____ . (hospital, hospitals)
3. It's in a big _____ . (city, cities)
4. It takes care of all kinds of _____ . (patient, patients)
5. It's near beautiful _____ . (mountain, mountains)
6. Apartment _____ are low. (rent, rents)

CONVERSATIONS

A. Which Job?

Gloria is talking to her father about the two job offers. He is writing down the information to help Gloria decide which job to take. Listen to the conversations and complete the information.

	City Hospital	General Hospital
Salary	$34,000	$27,000
Rent		
Transportation		
Hours (shift)		
Vacation		
Job		

B. How About?

To ask or find out more information, we often use *How about* or *What about*. Write the sentences you hear.

1. _____ _____ _____ _____ ?
2. _____ _____ _____ _____ ?
3. _____ _____ _____ _____ ?
4. _____ _____ _____ _____ ?
5. _____ _____ _____ _____ ?

C. Your Opinion

Which job do you think Gloria should take? Write three reasons. Share your reasons with the class.

Example: I think Gloria should take the job at City Hospital / General Hospital.

1. _____
2. _____
3. _____

INTERACTION

Sit with a partner. Ask your partner about his/her home. Ask your partner these questions and write his/her answers.

Question	My Partner's Answer
1. Where do you live?	
2. Do you live in a house or in an apartment?	
3. Is your neighborhood safe?	
4. Is your neighborhood clean?	
5. Is your neighborhood busy?	
6. Is your neighborhood noisy?	
7. Is your home near school?	
8. Is your home near town?	
9. Is your home near the bus or train?	
10. Is your home near work?	
11. Is your home near other family?	
12. Is your home near a park?	
13. Is the landlord helpful?	
14. Are the schools good?	
15. Are the neighbors friendly?	

A Bus Ride

COMPREHENSION

A. Discuss

Talk about these questions.

How far do you live from school?
How do you get to school?

B. Before You Listen

Many people take the bus to work or to school. What do people do when they are on the bus?

1. _____
2. _____
3. _____
4. _____

C. Key Words

Ask your teacher about any new words below. Listen to the sentences and fill in the correct words.

blind	offered
crowded	seeing-eye dog
angry	loud

1. The bus was so _____ that I couldn't find a seat.

2. His _____ helps him cross the street safely.

3. Please turn that music down. It's too _____ .

4. The young boy _____ the woman his seat.

5. Many _____ people wear dark glasses.

6. My boss gets _____ when I'm late for work.

🎞 D. First Listening

Debbie is taking the bus today. Look at the picture on page 20 and listen to the story as many times as you want. After you listen, tell the class any information you remember about the story.

🎞 E. Listen and Name

Listen to the story again. As you listen, write the name of each person on the picture.

Debbie	**Michael**	**Joanne**
Mrs. Wu	**Kathy**	**Kevin**

🎞 F. *Who* Questions

Answer these *Who* questions about the story. Write the name of the person on the line.

1. _____   4. _____

2. _____   5. _____

3. _____   6. _____

🎞 G. Comprehension Questions

Listen and circle the correct answer.

1. a. She always takes the bus.
   b. Her car is at the garage.
   c. She's late.
2. a. $ .25
   b. $1.25
   c. $1.50
3. a. Yes, she is.
   b. She's going to sit.
   c. She's going to stand.
4. a. She's late for work.
   b. The bus is crowded.
   c. She needs a cigarette.
5. a. No Smoking
   b. Exact Change Only
   c. Fire Exit
6. a. His dog is with him.
   b. He's going to work.
   c. He wants to get off at the right stop.
7. a. She's going to ask a friend for a ride.
   b. She's going to drive.
   c. She's going to take the bus.

> • *present continuous tense*
> • his / her

STRUCTURE

🔲 A. Listen and Write

Listen to these sentences. Write the present continuous verb you hear.

1. _____ is taking _____   6. _____
2. _____   7. _____
3. _____   8. _____
4. _____   9. _____
5. _____   10. _____

B. Read and Write

Complete these sentences about the story. Write the verb in the present continuous.

1. Debbie _____ on the bus. (get)
2. Lots of people _____ . (stand)
3. They _____ the bus to work. (take)
4. Mrs. Wu _____ for a seat. (look)
5. One boy _____ to his radio. (listen)
6. The bus _____ . (negative — move)
7. Joanne _____ to the sign in the front of the bus. (point)
8. Kevin _____ on the bus with his dog. (sit)
9. A woman _____ a man's wallet. (steal)
10. No one _____ . (watch)

PRONUNCIATION

🔲 A. *His* or *Her*

Listen to these sentences. Circle *his* or *her*.

1. his her   6. his her
2. his her   7. his her
3. his her   8. his her
4. his her   9. his her
5. his her   10. his her

CONVERSATIONS

🔲 A. Match

Listen to these conversations between people on the bus. Number each picture.

🔲 B. Place and Time

When we plan to meet a person, we often repeat the place and time to be sure we have the correct information. Listen to each statement. Fill in the exact place and time.

1. At the _____ at _____ .
2. In the _____ at _____ .
3. At the _____ at _____ .
4. By the _____ at _____ .
5. In _____ at _____ .
6. At your _____ at _____ .
7. On the _____ at _____ .
8. At the _____ at _____ .
9. At your _____ at _____ .
10. At the _____ at _____ .

🔲 C. Offering Help

In each conversation below, one person is offering help. Decide if the second person's answer means "Yes, thank you." or "No, thanks."
Circle *Yes* or *No*.

1. Yes   No   6. Yes   No
2. Yes   No   7. Yes   No
3. Yes   No   8. Yes   No
4. Yes   No   9. Yes   No
5. Yes   No   10. Yes   No

INTERACTION

In the box, draw a picture of yourself on your way to school. Sit in a small group and tell the other students about your picture. The other students will ask you the questions below.

1. Tell us about your picture. Where are you? What are you doing?
2. How far do you live from school?
3. How long does it take you to get to school?
4. Do you ever need a ride? Do you ever give someone else a ride?
5. Do you ever take public transportation?
6. Is it near your house?
7. How much is the fare? Do you need exact change?

THE SUPERMARKET

COMPREHENSION

A. Discuss

Talk about these questions.

> **Which supermarket do you shop at?**
> **How often do you go to the supermarket?**
> **How are the prices?**

B. Before You Listen

These are four departments in the supermarket. Write the names of four items you can buy in each department.

Produce	Bakery	Dairy	Meat

C. Key Words

Ask your teacher about any new words below. Listen to the sentences and fill in the correct words.

cart	bunch
aisle	adding
knocked over	angry

1. When he was running, the boy _____ some boxes of cookies.

2. When I go to the supermarket, my youngest child sits in the

   _____ .

3. He's buying a large _____ of grapes.

4. Where's the spaghetti? It's in _____ five.

5. My children are _____ more food to my cart.

6. She's _____ because her children are running around the store.

D. First Listening

Look at the pictures on page 26 and listen to the story as many times as you want. Mrs. Ryan has four children, Kelly, Marc, Tessa, and Jeff. What is each child doing? After you listen, tell the class any other information you remember about the story.

E. Listen and Choose

In the story, there are the names of many foods. Put a check before each item that is *in* Mrs. Ryan's cart.

_____ chicken   _____ cookies   _____ bananas

_____ cheese   _____ potato chips   _____ grapes

_____ ice cream   _____ doughnuts   _____ soda

F. Listen and Write the Letter

Listen to these sentences. Write the letter of the correct picture.

1. _____   5. _____
2. _____   6. _____
3. _____   7. _____
4. _____   8. _____

G. Comprehension Questions

Circle the correct answer.

1. a. at the supermarket
   b. on Friday night
   c. with her children
2. a. in the cart
   b. She's crying.
   c. She's the baby.
3. a. She's screaming.
   b. Yes, she is.
   c. She wants ice cream.
4. a. Yes, he is.
   b. No, he isn't.
   c. cookies and doughnuts
5. a. in the produce department
   b. a bunch of grapes
   c. She's eating.
6. a. soda
   b. aisle five
   c. Jeff knocked over some soda.
7. a. It's Friday night.
   b. Mrs. Ryan is leaving.
   c. Mrs. Ryan is smiling.

> • *present continuous tense*
> • *negatives*

STRUCTURE

🔲 A. Listen and Write

Listen to these sentences. Write the present continuous verb you hear.

1. ____are walking____   6. _____
2. _____   7. _____
3. _____   8. _____
4. _____   9. _____
5. _____   10. _____

B. Read and Write

Complete these sentences with a verb in the present continuous tense. Some of the sentences are negative.

1. Kelly _____ in the cart. (sit)

2. She _____ louder and louder. (cry)

3. Mrs. Ryan _____ to her. (listen)

4. Marc _____ his mother. (help)

5. He's putting food in the cart when she _____ . (look)

6. An employee _____ toward the manager. (walk)

7. She _____ a child with her. (pull)

8. Another employee _____ the floor. (mop)

9. Mrs. Ryan _____ out of the store. (walk)

10. She _____ at the manager. (smile)

PRONUNCIATION

🔲 A. Listen for Negatives

Listen to these sentences. Circle the verb you hear.

1. is smiling   isn't smiling   6. is watching   isn't watching

2. is putting   isn't putting   7. is pushing   isn't pushing

3. is looking   isn't looking   8. is eating   isn't eating

4. is screaming   isn't screaming   9. is talking   isn't talking

5. is listening   isn't listening   10. is walking   isn't walking

ANNOUNCEMENTS

A. Prices

Write the correct price. You will hear each price two times.

> forty-nine cents = $ .49 = 49¢
> a dollar thirty-nine = $1.39
> two for five dollars = 2 for $5.00 = 2/$5.00

1. _____   6. _____
2. _____   7. _____ /lb.
3. _____   8. _____ /lb.
4. _____   9. _____
5. _____   10. _____

B. Supermarket Announcements

Listen to these sale announcements. Find the item and write the sale price.

1. _____

2. _____

3. _____

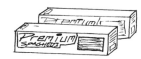

4. _____

5. _____

6. _____

C. Smart Shoppers

Paul and Susan are at the supermarket. They are checking prices to find the cheapest brand. Listen to their conversations, then circle the one they will buy.

1.

2.

3.

4.

5.

6.

7.

INTERACTION

As a class, decide on seven specific food items that you often buy in the supermarket. Be sure that you state the brand name and size, e.g. Best Pineapple Chunks (8 ounce can) or B&B Mayonnaise (1 quart jar). Write the names of the items in the chart below.

Choose three volunteers; each will go to a supermarket in the area. They will check the prices of these seven items. The three students will stand in front of the room with their price lists. The other students will ask the prices of the items. Listen carefully, and complete the chart.

Which supermarket has the best prices?

Items	Supermarkets		
1.			
2.			
3.			
4.			
5.			
6.			
7.			

THE DISCO

COMPREHENSION

A. Discuss

Talk about these questions.

> **Do you ever go to discos or clubs?**
> **Is there one in your city or town?**
> **What kind of music do they play?**
> **Is there a big dance floor?**
> **What's the cover charge?**

B. Before You Listen

This is **The Music Box,** Olga's favorite disco. Talk about the disco and the people. Write the vocabulary on the picture below: *band, bar, dance floor, dancing, partner.*

C. Key Words

Ask your teacher about any new words below. Listen to the sentences and fill in the correct words.

someone else	met
loud	favorite
over	partner

1. That man is a good dancer. His _____ is a great dancer!

2. I can't hear you! The music is too _____ .

3. I like many kinds of music, but my _____ is rock 'n roll.

4. He's not talking with his girlfriend. He's talking with _____ .

5. When the song is _____ , let's sit down.

6. She _____ a nice man at the disco last week.

31

📼 D. First Listening

Olga is at her favorite disco. Look at the pictures on page 32 and listen to the story as many times as you want. Who is Olga looking for? When did she first meet this person? After you listen, tell the class any other information you remember about the story.

📼 E. True or False

Read the statements, then listen to the story again. Write *T* if the statement is true. Write *F* if the statement is false.

_____ 1. Olga is drinking.

_____ 2. Olga is looking for her boyfriend.

_____ 3. Olga is standing with her friend.

_____ 4. Olga is looking for someone.

_____ 5. Olga is eating.

_____ 6. Olga is talking with her friends.

_____ 7. Olga is going home.

📼 F. Listen and Write the Letter

Listen to these sentences. Write the letter of the correct picture.

1. _____   5. _____

2. _____   6. _____

3. _____   7. _____

4. _____   8. _____

📼 G. Comprehension Questions

Listen and circle the correct answer.

1. a. It's a disco.   b. Yes, it is.   c. No, it isn't.

2. a. on the dance floor   b. She's talking.   c. at the bar

3. a. her boyfriend   b. someone special   c. her friend, Sonia

4. a. last night   b. last weekend   c. at the disco

5. a. No, she doesn't.   b. someone else   c. Yes, he is.

6. a. The song is over.   b. He isn't at the disco. c. He's dancing with someone else.

7. a. with her friends   b. on the dance floor   c. at home

> • *present continuous tense*
> • *statement or question*

STRUCTURE

A. Listen and Write

Listen to these sentences. Write the verb you hear. Some sentences are negative.

1. _____are standing_____   6. _____
2. _____   7. _____
3. _____   8. _____
4. _____   9. _____
5. _____   10. _____

B. Read and Write

Complete these sentences about the story. Write the verb in the present continuous.

1. Many people _____ . (eat)
2. Olga _____ . (eat - negative)
3. Olga _____ with her friend. (talk — negative)
4. She _____ for someone special. (look)
5. The band _____ a loud song. (play)
6. Lots of people _____ to the music. (dance)
7. The band _____ the next song. (begin)
8. He _____ toward her. (walk)
9. They _____ . (smile)

PRONUNCIATION

A. Statement or Question

Listen to these sentences about the story. Decide if each is a question or a statement. Circle *statement* or *question*.

1. statement   question   6. statement   question
2. statement   question   7. statement   question
3. statement   question   8. statement   question
4. statement   question   9. statement   question
5. statement   question   10. statement   question

CONVERSATIONS

🔲 A. Match

Listen to these four conversations about people at the disco. Number the men.

🔲 B. Which One?

Listen to these short phrases or sentences. Match each with the correct man. Write the number of the statement in the boxes under the correct picture.

🔲 C. Agree

Agree with each statement you hear. Circle the correct response.

1. a. Yes, he is.   b. Yes, she is.   c. Yes, it is.
2. a. Yes, he is.   b. Yes, she is.   c. Yes, it is.
3. a. Yes, he is.   b. Yes, she is.   c. Yes, it is.
4. a. Yes, he is.   b. Yes, she is.   c. Yes, it is.
5. a. Yes, he is.   b. Yes, she is.   c. Yes, it is.
6. a. Yes, he is.   b. Yes, she is.   c. Yes, it is.
7. a. Yes, he is.   b. Yes, she is.   c. Yes, it is.
8. a. Yes, he is.   b. Yes, she is.   c. Yes, it is.
9. a. Yes, he is.   b. Yes, she is.   c. Yes, it is.
10. a. Yes, he is.   b. Yes, she is.   c. Yes, it is.

INTERACTION

Sit with a partner. You are at a party together. You know a lot of people here; your friend doesn't know anyone. You are describing several people at the party. Make up three or four conversations about people at the party. Your teacher will walk around the class and help with any new vocabulary you need. Present one of your conversations to the class.

◣ **Example:**

A: That's my sister, the woman near the door.

B: The one with the big earrings?

A: No, the one with the sunglasses.

B: Is she wearing a short dress?

A: Yes, that's her.

VACATION

COMPREHENSION

A. Discuss

Talk about these questions.

Are you planning a vacation for this summer?
Where are you going to go?
What are you going to do there?
How long are you going to stay?

B. Before You Listen

Look at the map on page 38. Add these state names.

FLORIDA

NORTH CAROLINA

VIRGINIA

OHIO

C. Key Words

Ask your teacher about any new words below. Listen to the sentences and fill in the correct words.

camper	hike
directly	pack
full	ocean

1. We don't need gas. The tank is _____ .

2. Four people can sleep in our _____ .

3. Remember to _____ your sunglasses and a hat.

4. We're going _____ to Dallas; we're not going to stop anywhere.

5. They're going to _____ in the mountains.

6. In Florida, the _____ is warm. In California, it's cold.

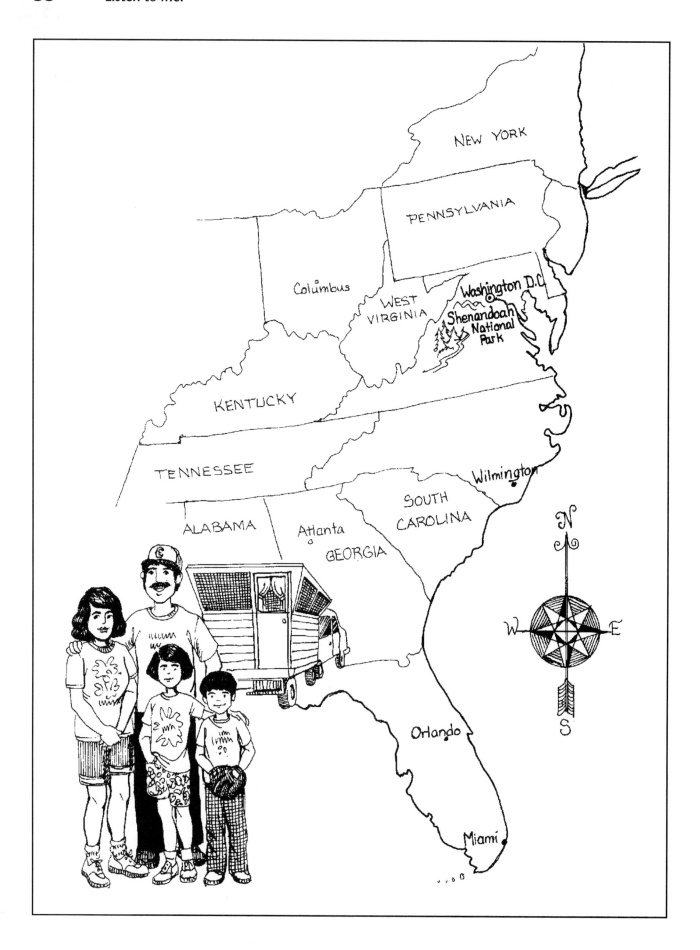

📼 D. First Listening

This family is going on vacation. Look at the map on page 38 and listen to the story. As you listen, draw their route on the map. After you listen, tell the class any information you remember about the story.

📼 E. Listen for Numbers

Read these questions about the story asking *How far* and *How long*. Then listen to the story again and answer with the questions.

1. How long are they going to be on vacation? _____

2. How far is it from Ohio to the Shenandoah National Park?
    _____

3. How long are they going to stay at the park? _____

4. How far is it from the park to Wilmington? _____

5. How long are they going to stay in North Carolina? _____

6. How far is it from Wilmington to Orlando? _____

7. How far are they staying from Disney World? _____

8. How far is it from Orlando back to Columbus? _____

📼 F. Comprehension Questions

Listen and circle the correct answer.

1. a. in Ohio   b. in Florida   c. in North Carolina
2. a. to Florida   b. tomorrow   c. by car
3. a. in motels   b. at night   c. in the camper
4. a. Yes, they did.   b. No, they didn't.
5. a. Yes, it is.   b. No, it isn't.
6. a. Yes, they are.   b. No, they aren't.
7. a. two days   b. 1,000 miles   c. nine hours

> • *future* going to *tense*
> • **for / from**
> • *question words*

STRUCTURE

🖭 A. Listen and Write

Listen to these sentences. Write the future verb you hear. In conversational English, *going to* sometimes sounds like *gonna*.

1. _____are going to leave_____   6. _____
2. _____   7. _____
3. _____   8. _____
4. _____   9. _____
5. _____   10. _____

PRONUNCIATION

🖭 A. *For* or *From*

Listen to these sentences. Circle the preposition you hear.

1. for   from   6. for   from
2. for   from   7. for   from
3. for   from   8. for   from
4. for   from   9. for   from
5. for   from   10. for   from

🖭 B. Question Words

Listen to these questions about vacations. Write the question word(s).

1. _____   6. _____
2. _____   7. _____
3. _____   8. _____
4. _____   9. _____
5. _____   10. _____

CONVERSATIONS

A. Vacations

Listen to these conversations about summer vacation plans. Fill in the chart below. Write where each person(s) is going and how long each is going to stay there. If you don't know the information, put a **?**.

Conversation	Where	How long
1		
2		
3		
4		
5		
6		

B. Yes or No

In conversational English, many words and sounds mean *yes* or *no*. Listen to the examples. Then, listen to these questions and answers. Decide if the answer means *yes* or *no*. Circle *yes* or *no*.

Yes	No
Yeah	Nope
Yup	Nah
Uh-huh	Uh-uh
Hmm-Hmm	No way

1. yes   no
2. yes   no
3. yes   no
4. yes   no
5. yes   no

6. yes   no
7. yes   no
8. yes   no
9. yes   no
10. yes   no

C. Repeating

In conversation, the listener often repeats the last word or phrase of the speaker, using question intonation. This shows the listener is interested or surprised and would like more information.

Example 1:   A: I'm going to visit my sister in Santa Fe.
            B: Santa Fe?

Example 2:   A: I'm going to be right here.
            B: Here?

Listen to each speaker's summer plans. Then write the last word or phrase you hear.

1. _____ ?
2. _____ ?
3. _____ ?
4. _____ ?
5. _____ ?

6. _____ ?
7. _____ ?
8. _____ ?
9. _____ ?
10. _____ ?

INTERACTION

You have two weeks for vacation. These pictures show several popular vacation areas. Where would you like to go? Circle two places.

Sit in a small group. Tell the other students which places you chose and why. Answer the questions they ask you about your first choice.

1. Where are you going to go?

2. Who are you going to go with?

3. When are you going to go?

4. How are you going to get there?

5. How long are you going to stay there?

6. What are you going to do there?

7. What preparations are you going to make?

8. How much money are you going to bring?

EDUARDO

COMPREHENSION

A. Discuss

Talk about these questions.

> **Are you going to visit or return to your native country
> at some time in the future?**
> **What are your plans?**
> **How much is an airline ticket from here to your country?**

B. Before You Listen

Eduardo is packing his suitcase. He's going to visit his native country, Colombia. What do you think he's bringing?

C. Key Words

Ask your teacher about any new words below. Listen to the sentences and fill in the correct words.

lonely	packing
serious	alone
together	at first

1. I live _____ in a small apartment.

2. He's _____ his clothes and the presents he's bringing.

3. _____ , he didn't speak any English.

4. Sometimes when I think of my family, I feel _____ .

5. He's getting _____ about a girl from his native country.

6. They're going to go to the beach _____ .

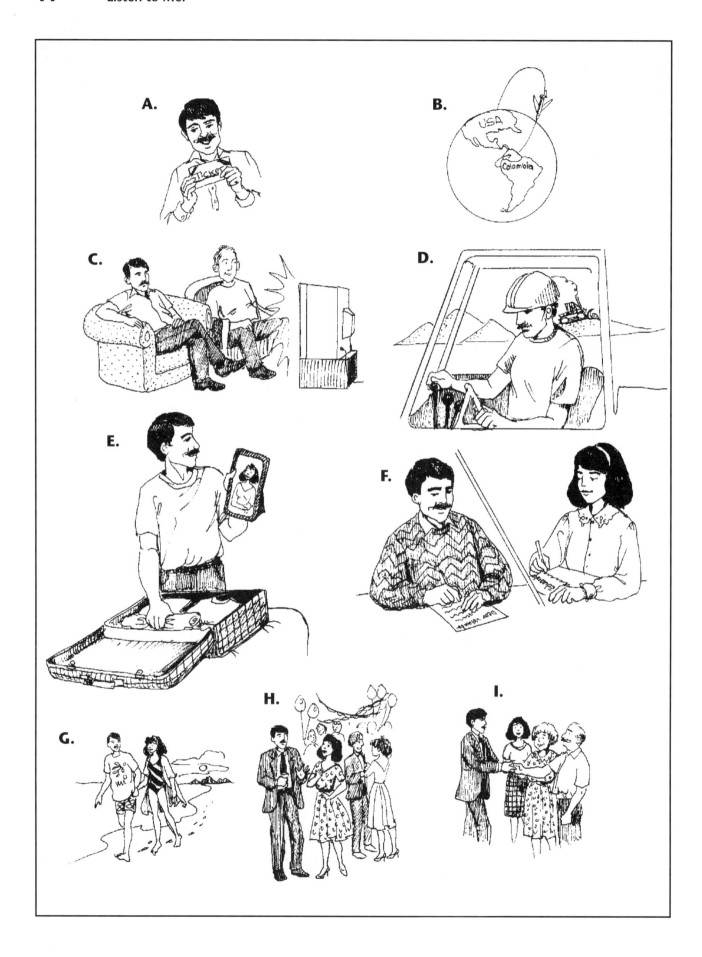

🔊 D. First Listening

Eduardo is returning to his native country for a visit. Look at the pictures on page 44 and listen to the story as many times as you want. After you listen, tell the class any information you remember about the story.

🔊 E. Listen and Write the Letter

Listen to these sentences. Write the letter of the correct picture.

1. _____   5. _____

2. _____   6. _____

3. _____   7. _____

4. _____   8. _____

🔊 F. Listen and Choose

Read the sentences below, then listen to the story again. Put a check in front of the things Eduardo is going to do in Colombia.

_____ 1. He's going to tell his family about his life in the United States.

_____ 2. He's going to work hard.

_____ 3. He's going to walk on the beach.

_____ 4. He's going to look for an apartment.

_____ 5. He's going to visit Yolanda's family.

_____ 6. He's going to go to parties.

_____ 7. He's going to write to Yolanda.

🔊 G. Comprehension Questions

Listen and circle the correct answer.

1. a. tomorrow   b. winter   c. summer

2. a. in Colombia   b. in the United States   c. for three years

3. a. a cousin   b. in a small apartment   c. a friend

4. a. He works hard.   b. His family is in   c. He lives alone.
                             Colombia.

5. a. three years ago   b. a month   c. tomorrow

6. a. three years ago   b. a month   c. tomorrow

7. a. They went to high   b. They went to college   c. He worked with
      school together.   together.   her in New Jersey.

> • *future* going to *tense*
> • her / him / them

STRUCTURE

🔲 **A. Listen and Write**

Listen to these sentences. Write the future tense verb you hear.

1. _____ is going to leave _____
2. _____
3. _____
4. _____
5. _____
6. _____
7. _____
8. _____
9. _____
10. _____

PRONUNCIATION

🔲 **A.** *Her / His / Him*

Listen to these sentences. Complete them with *her*, *his*, or *him*. Note that the *h* is often silent.

1. He's packing _____ suitcase.

2. He's going to visit _____ family.

3. He's looking at _____ picture.

4. He's going to see _____ tomorrow.

5. She's going to be happy to see _____ .

6. He's going to talk to _____ about the future.

7. She's going to take _____ to a family party.

8. He's going to buy _____ a ring.

9. He's going to ask _____ to marry _____ .

10. She's going to go back to the United States with _____ .

CONVERSATIONS

A. Match

Yolanda and Eduardo are in love. They are talking about life in the United States. Listen to these three conversations. Match each conversation with Yolanda's feelings.

_____ 1. Yolanda wants to marry Eduardo and come to the United States.

_____ 2. Yolanda isn't sure she wants to live in the United States.

_____ 3. Yolanda doesn't want to leave Colombia.

B. *Can / Can't*

Listen to these sentences. Complete them with *can* or *can't* and the verb.

1. I _____ _____ to school.

2. I _____ _____ Colombia.

3. I _____ _____ a job.

4. I _____ _____ back to Colombia.

5. I _____ _____ English.

6. I _____ _____ letters.

7. I _____ _____ my aunt and uncle.

C. Interested?

Two people are discussing plans for the next week. The first person is making a suggestion. Decide if the second person is interested or not. Check *Interested* or *Not Interested*.

	Interested	*Not interested*
1.	_____	_____
2.	_____	_____
3.	_____	_____
4.	_____	_____
5.	_____	_____
6.	_____	_____
7.	_____	_____

INTERACTION

Your cousin is planning to come to live in the United States. What is she going to like about life in the United States? What isn't she going to like? Work alone and write two sentences about each. Then share your ideas with a small group. Add more ideas to your list.

Things she is going to like:

1. _____

2. _____

3. _____

4. _____

5. _____

6. _____

Things she isn't going to like:

1. _____

2. _____

3. _____

4. _____

5. _____

6. _____

DIVORCE

9

COMPREHENSION

A. Discuss

Talk about these questions.

> **Do you know anyone who is divorced?**
> **Do they have children?**
> **Do the children live with their mother or with their father?**
> **How often do they see the other parent?**

B. Before You Listen

Why do you think these boys are upset? How do their parents feel? What do you think they are talking about?

C. Key Words

Ask your teacher about any new words below. Listen to the sentences and fill in the correct words.

far	anymore
near	argue
anytime	together

1. My sister and her husband _____ about money, the car, the children, everything.

2. They don't love each other _____ .

3. Their parents are living _____ away in another state.

4. You can call me _____ ; I'll always have time to talk to you.

5. My sister lives _____ me in the same town.

6. We're going on vacation _____ in the summer.

49

D. First Listening

Tom and Marsha are going to get a divorce. Look at the pictures on page 50 and listen to the story as many times as you want. After you listen, tell the class any information you remember about the story.

E. Listen and Write the Letter

Listen to these sentences. Write the letter of the correct picture.

1. _____   5. _____

2. _____   6. _____

3. _____   7. _____

4. _____   8. _____

F. True or False

Read these statements about the story. Write *T* if the statement is true, *F* if the statement is false.

_____ 1. Tom and Marsha love each other very much.

_____ 2. Tom and Marsha are having problems with their children.

_____ 3. Tom and Marsha love their children very much.

_____ 4. Tom is going to move far away.

_____ 5. Tom wants to see his sons often.

G. Comprehension Questions

Listen and circle the correct answer.

1. a. the boys   b. money   c. I don't know.

2. a. in the kitchen   b. ten and eight   c. They're sad.

3. a. a new school   b. the same school   c. I don't know.

4. a. this weekend   b. near   c. to an apartment

5. a. to the next town   b. this weekend   c. I don't know.

6. a. two weekends   b. anytime   c. in his apartment
   a month

7. a. every weekend   b. twice a month   c. anytime

> • *future* going to *tense*
> • *tense contrast*
> • *time expressions*

STRUCTURE

A. Listen and Write

Listen to these sentences. Write the future tense verb you hear. In spoken English, *going to* sounds like *gonna*.

1. _____are going to get_____   6. _____

2. _____   7. _____

3. _____   8. _____

4. _____   9. _____

5. _____   10. _____

B. Listen for Tense

Listen to these sentences. Decide if the verb is about right now or the future. Circle *right now* or *future*.

1. right now   future   6. right now   future

2. right now   future   7. right now   future

3. right now   future   8. right now   future

4. right now   future   9. right now   future

5. right now   future   10. right now   future

C. Time Expressions

Listen to these sentences. Fill in the time expression.

1. The boys are going to see their father _____ .

2. They call him _____ .

3. They're going to go on vacation _____ .

4. Tom and Marsha argue _____ .

5. Tom is going to leave _____ .

6. He's going to move _____ .

7. The boys are going to see their father _____ .

8. They're going to call their father _____ .

9. Marsha is going to talk to a lawyer _____ .

10. Tom is going to look for an apartment _____ .

CONVERSATIONS

🔲 A. Match

Listen to each argument. Decide what the man and woman are arguing about. Number each picture.

🔲 B. Listen for Stress

The most important word or words in a sentence are stressed. These words are the loudest and strongest in the sentence. Listen and circle the word or words that are stressed.

◢ **Example:** You (never) do (anything.)

1. You always say that.
2. You do nothing.
3. You just sit in front of the TV.
4. You're no help at all.
5. I do everything.

6. You're an hour late.
7. I needed a coat.
8. And I needed a camera.
9. You never think about me.
10. It's always what you want.

C. Stress

In each short conversation, two people are arguing. Sit with a partner and try these conversations together. Stress the most important words.

1. A: I can't help you.
   B: Why not?
   A: I'm tired.
   B: You're always tired.

2. A: You never help with the shopping.
   B: I hate the supermarket.
   A: I don't like it, either.
   B: I'll come next time.
   A: That's your favorite expression. Next time.

3. A: What's for dinner?
   B: I don't know.
   A: You don't know?
   B: I'm not cooking.
   A: You're not?
   B: I cleaned all day. You watched TV. Now, I think I'll watch TV.

INTERACTION

1. Sit with a partner and share your ideas. What are some of the things that people argue about? Put more ideas in this box.

money   clothes

noise   children

Who do you argue with . . . someone in your family? a friend? a neighbor? Complete these sentences, then share the information with your partner.

a. I sometimes argue with my _____ . We argue about

_____ .

b. I sometimes argue with my _____ . We argue about

_____ .

c. I sometimes argue with my _____ . We argue about

_____ .

2. Make up a short argument between two people. Present it to the class. Then the class can try to guess who is arguing: a parent and child, two neighbors, a brother and sister, a husband and wife, etc.

ANA AND PETER

COMPREHENSION

A. Discuss

Talk about these questions.

> **What is a housewife?**
> **What is a househusband?**
> **In most families with children, does one of the parents stay home or do they both work?**

B. Before You Listen

Answer these questions about your own family.

1. Who cleans the house?

2. Who does the laundry?

3. Who does the food shopping?

4. Who cooks?

5. Who irons the clothes?

C. Key Words

Ask your teacher about any new words below. Listen to the sentences and fill in the correct words.

shuttle		nap	
still		flight	
spend time		miss	

1. _____ 963 is going to land at 4:46.

2. When my wife is away on business, I _____ her.

3. I _____ with my children in the evening.

4. She isn't home yet; she's _____ at work.

5. In the afternoon, I put my youngest child in bed for a _____ .

6. The _____ between New York and Boston leaves every hour.

A.

B.

C.

D.

E.

F.

G.

H.

D. First Listening

Look at the pictures on page 56 and listen to the story about Ana and Peter as many times as you want. After you listen, tell the class any information you remember about the story.

E. Listen and Write the Letter

Listen to these sentences. Write the letter of the correct picture.

1. _____   5. _____
2. _____   6. _____
3. _____   7. _____
4. _____   8. _____

F. Listen and Choose

Ana and Peter have busy lives. Put an A in front of Ana's activities. Put a P in front of Peter's activities.

_____   1. flies the daily shuttle from New York to Boston

_____   2. gets the children ready for school

_____   3. does the food shopping

_____   4. has a small business at home

_____   5. helps the children with their homework

_____   6. reads to the children

_____   7. leaves the house early in the morning

_____   8. does the laundry

_____   9. makes dinner

_____ 10. cleans the house

G. Comprehension Questions

Listen and circle the correct answer.

1. a. 6:30 A.M.   b. 6:00 P.M.   c. 8:00 P.M.

2. a. Ana   b. Peter   c. the baby-sitter

3. a. Yes, he does.   b. Yes, he is.   c. It's a lot of work.

4. a. He cleans.   b. He takes a nap.   c. He fixes TVs.

5. a. in the morning   b. in the afternoon   c. in the evening

6. a. in the morning   b. on the telephone   c. after the children
                                                    go to bed

7. a. The flight is going b. She misses him.   c. She's worried.
       to be late.

> • *present tense*
> • *pronunciation of* s

STRUCTURE

🔲 A. Listen and Write

Listen to these sentences. Write the present tense verb you hear.

1. _____gets up_____   6. _____
2. _____   7. _____
3. _____   8. _____
4. _____   9. _____
5. _____   10. _____

PRONUNCIATION

🔲 A. Same or Different

You will hear two verbs. Decide if they are the same or different. Circle *same* or *different*.

1. same   different   6. same   different
2. same   different   7. same   different
3. same   different   8. same   different
4. same   different   9. same   different
5. same   different   10. same   different

🔲 B. Pronunciation of s

Listen to the pronunciation of these verbs.

/s/	/z/	/ɪz/
eats	says	dresses
likes	cleans	fixes

Look at the verbs below. Listen to the pronunciation of s. Circle the pronunciation you hear.

1. takes   /s/   /z/   /ɪz/   6. reads   /s/   /z/   /ɪz/
2. has   /s/   /z/   /ɪz/   7. relaxes   /s/   /z/   /ɪz/
3. enjoys   /s/   /z/   /ɪz/   8. shops   /s/   /z/   /ɪz/
4. looks   /s/   /z/   /ɪz/   9. watches   /s/   /z/   /ɪz/
5. misses   /s/   /z/   /ɪz/   10. stays   /s/   /z/   /ɪz/

CONVERSATIONS

📼 A. Match

Listen to these conversations between Peter and his children. Number each picture.

📼 B. *Like / Don't like*

Listen to these short conversations. Give your opinion. Complete *one* of each pair of sentences. Don't worry about spelling.

▲ **Example:** Good, I like _____pizza_____. Oh, I don't like _____.

1. Good, I like _____. Oh, I don't like _____.
2. Good, I like _____. Oh, I don't like _____.
3. Good, I like _____. Oh, I don't like _____.
4. Good, I like _____. Oh, I don't like _____.
5. Good, I like _____. Oh, I don't like _____.
6. Good, I like _____. Oh, I don't like _____.
7. Good, I like _____. Oh, I don't like _____.
8. Good, I like _____. Oh, I don't like _____.
9. Good, I like _____. Oh, I don't like _____.
10. Good, I like _____. Oh, I don't like _____.

🔲 C. Short Answers

Listen carefully for *he* or *she* in these questions. Circle the correct answer.

1. a. Yes, he does.   b. Yes, she does.
2. a. No, he doesn't.   b. No, she doesn't.
3. a. Yes, he does.   b. Yes, she does.
4. a. Yes, he does.   b. Yes, she does.
5. a. Yes, he does.   b. Yes, she does.
6. a. No, he doesn't.   b. No, she doesn't.
7. a. Yes, he does.   b. Yes, she does.
8. a. No, he doesn't.   b. No, she doesn't.
9. a. Yes, he does.   b. Yes, she does.
10. a. No, he doesn't.   b. No, she doesn't.

INTERACTION

1. Taking care of a house or apartment is a lot of work. Sit with a small group and talk about the chores below. Which do you like to do? Which don't you like to do?

2. Discuss this situation with your group.

Katie and Mark were married last month. They are 25 years old. They both work; they leave the house about 7:00 A.M. and get home about 5:00 P.M. Which chores should Katie do? Which chores should Mark do? Two or three groups should present their ideas to the class.

VOLUNTEERS

COMPREHENSION

A. Discuss

Talk about these questions.

What is a volunteer?
Do you volunteer in your church, temple, child's school, community, etc.?
What do you do?

B. Before You Listen

Where can people do volunteer work? What do the volunteers do?

_____

_____

_____

_____

C. Key Words

Ask your teacher about any new words below. Listen to the sentences and fill in the correct words.

team	alcoholic
meal	Recreation
infants	coach

1. Sometimes it is difficult for older people to prepare a hot _____ for themselves.

2. A soccer _____ has 11 players.

3. The _____ Department in our town has many sports programs for children.

4. _____ need a lot of love and attention.

5. If a mother is an _____ , her baby often has physical problems.

6. The _____ wants the boys to practice more.

INFANT CARE
UNIT

🔊 D. First Listening

Listen to this story about three volunteers. Match each name below and the volunteer work each person does. After you listen, tell the class any information you remember about the story.

1. __C__ Walter   a. a soccer coach

2. __a__ Tom   b. a cuddler

3. __b__ Kate   c. a driver for "Meals on Wheels"

🔊 E. Listen and Decide

Listen to these sentences about the volunteers in the story.
Circle *Walter*, *Tom*, or *Kate*.

1. Walter   Tom   Kate

2. Walter   Tom   Kate

3. Walter   Tom   Kate

4. Walter   Tom   Kate

5. Walter   Tom   Kate

6. Walter   Tom   Kate

7. Walter   Tom   Kate

8. Walter   Tom   Kate

🔊 F. Comprehension Questions

Listen and circle the correct answer.

1. a. a few hours   b. over 50 percent   c. in their communities

2. a. at lunch time   b. to senior citizens   c. at church

3. a. They're old.   b. They're alone.   c. They have physical problems.

4. a. Yes, he is.   b. the coach   c. his son

5. a. on Saturdays   b. at school   c. one afternoon a week

6. a. They're sick.   b. They're drug users.   c. in the Infant Care Unit

7. a. She has AIDS.   b. No, she isn't.   c. She gives them love.

> • *present tense*
> • *of*

STRUCTURE

🎧 **A. Listen and Write**

Listen to these sentences. Write the present tense verb you hear.

1. ___volunteer___
2. _____
3. _____
4. _____
5. _____

6. _____
7. _____
8. _____
9. _____
10. _____

B. Read and Write

Complete these sentences from the story with a verb in the present tense.

1. Walter _____ hot meals. (deliver)
2. He _____ to 11 homes in his town. (drive)
3. Most of the people _____ alone. (live)
4. Walter _____ for a few minutes. (talk)
5. Each team _____ one afternoon a week. (practice)
6. On Saturday, the teams _____ one another. (play)
7. Kate _____ at Children's Hospital. (volunteer)
8. Some of the children _____ AIDS. (have)
9. Kate _____ the babies. (hold)
10. Kate says, "I _____ them love." (give)

PRONUNCIATION

🎧 **A. Of (All of, Most of, Many of, Some of, A few of, None of)**

Listen and complete these sentences. The word *of* is often reduced. We do not say or hear the *f*. Listen to this example.

▲ **Example: Some of the volunteers work in the morning.**

1. _____ ____ ____ _____ are older.
2. _____ ____ ____ _____ have AIDS.
3. _____ ____ ____ _____ enjoy their work.
4. _____ ____ ____ _____ live alone.
5. _____ ____ ____ _____ have physical problems.

6. _____ ___ ___ _____ get paid.

7. ___ ___ ___ ___ _____ work in the evening.

8. ___ ___ ___ _____ need love.

9. _____ ___ ___ _____ are alcoholics.

10. _____ ___ ___ _____ play on Sunday.

CONVERSATIONS

🔲 A. Match

Listen to these six people talk about their volunteer work. Number each picture.

🔲 B. Listen for Days and Times

Listen to the conversations again. Fill in the days and/or time that each person volunteers.

Conversation	Days and Times
1	
2	
3	
4	
5	
6	

🔊 C. Listen for Prepositions

Listen to these sentences from the story. Complete them with the correct preposition.

1. He sings _____ the choir _____ church.
2. They meet _____ Wednesday.
3. They practice _____ 8:00 _____ 10:00.
4. He sings _____ the 9:00 service.
5. She gives time _____ Monday night.
6. She volunteers _____ 8:00 _____ 12:00.
7. She works _____ the library _____ her daughter's school.
8. He works _____ a soup kitchen _____ his house.
9. She volunteers _____ a nursing home.
10. She goes there _____ Friday afternoons.

INTERACTION

You have two hours a week and would like to volunteer. Check one or two activities below that interest you. Share your interests with your group. Why would you enjoy this activity?

deliver "Meals on Wheels"	___
coach a sport	___
work with infants	___
join the Rescue Squad	___
teach a child or an adult how to read	___
visit people who are sick	___
cook in a soup kitchen	___
work in a library	___
work with children with disabilities	___
work at a blood bank	___
other: _____	___

I'd like to _____ .

I wouldn't like to _____ .

GOOD HEALTH

COMPREHENSION

A. Discuss

Talk about these questions.

> **What is a heart attack?**
> **Do you know anyone who had a heart attack?**
> **What are the causes of a heart attack?**

B. Before You Listen

Heart attack is the number one cause of death in the United States for both men and women. Heart attacks are not usually caused by one factor, but by a number of factors together. How many of these factors do you have?

Do you smoke?	Yes	No
Do you have high cholesterol?	Yes	No
Do you have high blood pressure?	Yes	No
Do you have diabetes?	Yes	No
Are you overweight?	Yes	No
Do you have a lot of stress?	Yes	No
Do you need to exercise more?	Yes	No
Do you have a family history of heart attacks?	Yes	No

C. Key Words

Ask your teacher about any new words below. Listen to the sentences and fill in the correct words.

turned 50	collapsed
except	increase
cardiac	dizzy

1. My father _____ on his last birthday.

2. When he had his heart attack, the man _____ on the floor.

3. Many hospitals have _____ units to care for patients with heart problems.

4. No one in my family smokes, _____ me.

5. You can walk one mile the first month. The second month, you can _____ that to two miles.

6. When it's very hot in a room, I sometimes feel _____ .

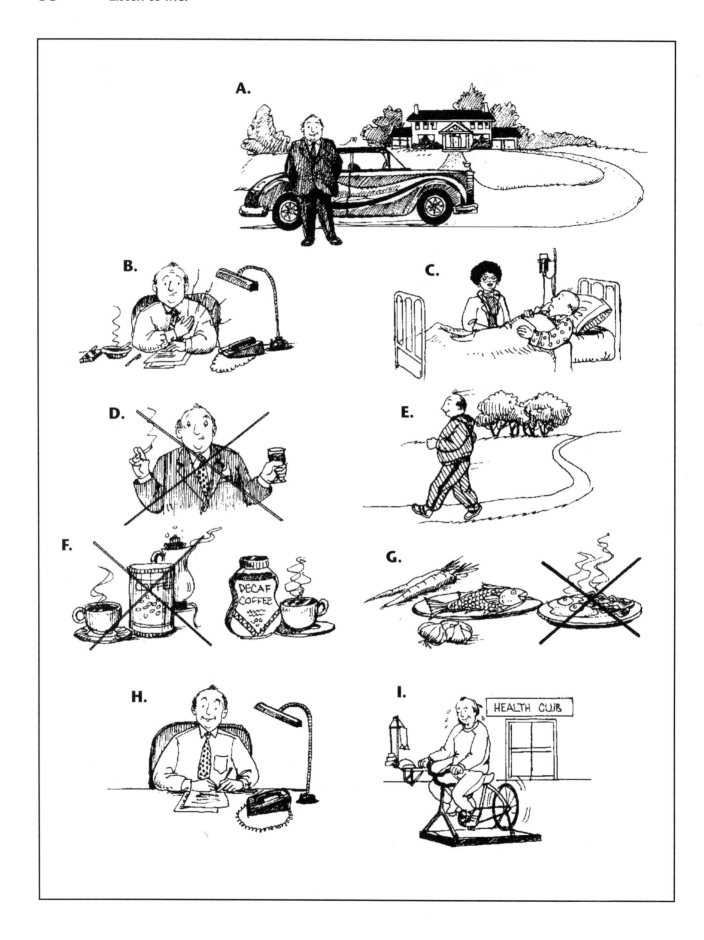

▭ **D. First Listening**

Look at the pictures on page 68 and listen to the story about Len as many times as you want. After you listen, tell the class any information you remember about the story.

▭ **E. Listen and Write the Letter**

Listen to these sentences. Write the letter of the correct picture.

1. _____   5. _____

2. _____   6. _____

3. _____   7. _____

4. _____   8. _____

▭ **F. Listen and Choose**

Read the instructions below, then listen to the story again. Put a check in front of each of the doctor's orders for Len.

_____ 1. lose weight

_____ 2. walk a mile in the morning

_____ 3. eat at fast food restaurants

_____ 4. work eight hours a day

_____ 5. eat more vegetables

_____ 6. drink regular coffee

_____ 7. slow down at the office

▭ **G. Comprehension Questions**

Listen and circle the correct answer.

1. a. He's sick.   b. He's 50.   c. Yes, he is.

2. a. He had a heart   b. It was his birthday.   c. He was leaving his
      attack.   office.

3. a. He didn't take   b. He felt dizzy.   c. He has to slow
      care of himself.   down.

4. a. the doctor   b. the cardiac care unit   c. for two weeks

5. a. steak   b. vegetables   c. fish

6. a. before work   b. after work   c. before and after
                                                             work

7. a. four   b. seven   c. eight

> • *present tense*
> • **can / can't**

STRUCTURE

🔲 A. Listen and Write

Listen to these sentences. Write the present tense verb you hear.

1. _____is_____   6. _____
2. _____   7. _____
3. _____   8. _____
4. _____   9. _____
5. _____ 10. _____

🔲 B. Listen for Modals

Listen to these sentences. Write the complete verb you hear. Listen for *has to*, *can*, or *can't*.

▲ **Examples:**   A: He ___has to watch___ his diet.
           B: He ___can eat___ chicken and fish.
           C: He ___can't eat___ steak.

1. He ___has to lose___ weight.
2. He ___can't drink___ regular coffee.
3. He ___has to drink___ decaf coffee.
4. He ___can't put___ salt on his food.
5. He ___has to exercise___ before and after work.
6. He ___has to join___ a health club.
7. He ___can't smoke___ anymore.
8. He ___can go back___ to work next month.
9. He ___has to slow down___ at the office.
10. He ___can't work___ ten hours a day anymore.

PRONUNCIATION

🔲 A. Short Answers

Listen to these questions about the story. Answer with *Yes, he can.* or *No, he can't.*

1. _No, he can't_   6. _yes, he can_
2. _No, he can't_   7. _No, he can't_
3. _yes, he can_   8. _yes, he can_
4. _No, he can't_   9. _yes, he can_
5. _No, he can't_   10. _No, he can't_

CONVERSATIONS

🔲 A. Match

Len is at the doctor for his three-month checkup. Listen to these conversations between Len and his doctor. Number each picture.

🔲 B. Conversation Questions

Listen to the conversations again. Answer these questions with the class.

1. How many times a day should Len take his medication?

2. What does the doctor mean when he says, "You were lucky this time?"

3. How many more hours can Len work this month?

4. How many cups of regular coffee can Len have a day? How many cups of decaf?

5. How many minutes will it take Len to walk two miles?

6. Is Len's cholesterol still too high?

🔲 C. Same or Different

Read each sentence. Then, listen to the sentence on the tape. Decide if the meaning of the two sentences is the same or different. Circle *same* or *different*.

1. You can smoke one cigarette a day.   same   different

2. I want to work eight hours a day.   same   different

3. You can work five hours a day this month. same   different

4. Before your heart attack, you drank six
   or seven cups of coffee a day.   same   different

5. A regular cup of coffee.   same   different

6. You lost weight.   same   different

7. Tomorrow, you can walk two miles.   same   different

8. Your cholesterol level is up.   same   different

9. You can eat steak and eggs.   same   different

10. I understand you.   same   different

D. The Doctor's Orders

These are the doctor's orders. Check the sentence you hear.

1. ___ Take this once a day.

   ___ Take this twice a day.

2. ___ Take one tablet with each meal.

   ___ Take one tablet before each meal.

3. ___ Take one to four tablets as needed for pain.

   ___ Take one tablet every four hours as needed for pain.

4. ___ Take three tablets three times a day.

   ___ Take three tablets now, then one tablet three times a day.

5. ___ Take one tablet one hour after each meal.

   ___ Take one tablet after each meal.

6. ___ Take two tablespoonfuls before you go to bed.

   ___ Take two teaspoonfuls before you go to bed.

7. ___ Take a half teaspoonful three times a day.

   ___ Take one and a half teaspoonfuls three times a day.

INTERACTION

Sit with a partner. In the columns below, make a list of everything you ate
and drank yesterday. Check each list. Cross out all the foods that a person
with heart trouble should not eat or drink. For each item you crossed out,
substitute a food that is healthy.

Breakfast	Lunch	Dinner	Snacks

FAST THINKING

COMPREHENSION

A. Discuss

Talk about these questions.

Did anyone ever rob you?
What happened?
What did the person steal?
Did you call the police?
What did they do?

B. Before You Listen

Look at this picture from the story. What is the man doing? What is the woman with the two boys doing? What do you think she is going to do?

C. Key Words

Ask your teacher about any new words below. Listen to the sentences and fill in the correct words.

focused	film
scream	was stealing
robbery	arrested

1. Last night, there was a _____ at our friend's house.

2. The police _____ the man who stole my money.

3. He _____ the camera to get a better picture of the children.

4. I jumped out of bed when I heard a loud _____ .

5. Last week, I saw a woman who _____ a sweater from a store.

6. This roll of _____ takes 24 pictures.

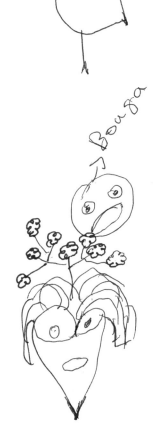

📼 **D. First Listening**

Look at the pictures on page 74 and listen to the story about a robbery as many times as you want. After you listen, tell the class any information you remember about the story.

📼 **E. Listen and Choose**

Read the statements below, then listen to the story again. Put a check in front of the information you know about the robber.

- ✓ 1. He was sitting under a tree.
- _____ 2. He took Sally's camera.
- ✓ 3. He took a woman's purse.
- ✓ 4. He ran away.
- _____ 5. He took a picture of Sally.
- ✓ 6. His picture was in the newspaper.
- ✓ 7. He's now in jail.

📼 **F. Listen and Write the Letter**

Listen to these sentences. Write the letter of the correct picture.

1. G   6. A
2. D   7. D
3. E   8. B
4. F   9. I
5. C   10. H

📼 **G. Listen and Decide**

You will hear a sentence from the story. Decide what happened after that. Circle the correct answer.

1. ✓a. They talked and read.   b. Sally focused her camera.

2. a. She took out her camera.   b. She thought fast.

3. a. The police came.   ✓b. She looked up.

4. ✓a. She heard a scream.   b. She took three pictures of him.

5. ✓a. She gave them the film.   b. They arrested the man.

6. ✓a. The photograph was in the newspaper.   b. The police went to his house.

7. ✓a. They knew his address.   ✓b. They arrested him.

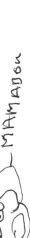

- *past tense (irregular verbs)*
- *tense contrast*

STRUCTURE

🔲 A. Listen and Write

Listen to these sentences. Write the past tense verb you hear.

1. _____sat_____   6. ___took___
2. ___read___   7. ___came___
3. ___Took___   8. ___was___
4. ___heard___   9. ___knew___
5. ___Thought___   10. ___went___

🔲 B. Tense Contrast

Listen to these sentences. Decide the tense of the verb. Circle *present*, *past*, or *future*.

1. (present)   past   future   6. present   (past)   future
2. (present)   past   future   7. (present)   past   future
3. present   (past)   future   8. present   past   (future)
4. present   (past)   future   9. present   past   (future)
5. present   past   (future)   10. present   (past)   future

PRONUNCIATION

🔲 A. Listen and Circle

You will hear two verbs. Decide if they are the same or different. Circle *same* or *different*.

1. same   (different)   6. (same)   different
2. same   (different)   7. same   (different)
3. same   (different)   8. same   (different)
4. same   (different)   9. (same)   different
5. (same)   different   10. same   (different)

CONVERSATIONS

A. Which One?

This morning, the police arrested John at his apartment. The neighbors are talking about the event. Which neighbors have a newspaper? Put a check after those conversations.

Conversation 1 _____

Conversation 2 ✓_____

Conversation 3 ✓_____

Conversation 4 _____

B. Surprise

In each conversation there is an expression of surprise. Listen to the conversations again and write the letter(s) of the expression(s) you hear.

Conversation   *Expression*

1. _____   a. Really?

2. _____ _____   b. You're not serious!

3. _____   c. I can't believe it!

4. _____   d. That's hard to believe!

                                        e. You're kidding!

C. Question or Statement

Listen to these sentences about the story. Decide if each is a question or a statement. Circle *statement* or *question*.

Examples: STATEMENT: **John robbed a woman.**
                  QUESTION: **John robbed a woman?**

1. statement   question   6. statement   question

2. statement   question   7. statement   question

3. statement   question   8. statement   question

4. statement   question   9. statement   question

5. statement   question   10. statement   question

D. Dictation

Listen and write these questions.

1. What did he do ?
2. Why did he do it ?
3. What did he stil ?
4. Whent did The police come ?
5. Where did you hear about This ?
6. What did The police do ?

INTERACTION

Sally always takes her camera with her. Do you have a camera? What do you like to take pictures of? Share your list with a small group.

I like to take pictures of...

- my son playing soccer
- my father on his motorcycle
- my children on their birthdays

Bring in two or three pictures you took. Tell your group about the people and the occasion.

THE ACCIDENT

COMPREHENSION

A. Discuss

Talk about these questions.

> **Were you ever in a car accident?**
> **What happened?**
> **Was anyone hurt?**
> **Was there any damage to the cars?**

B. Before You Listen

Read these statements about motor vehicle accidents in the United States. Write *T* if the statement is true, *F* if the statement is false. Then check your answers on page 80.

__T__ 1. Most accidents happen less than ten miles from home.

__T__ 2. Every day, there are about 18,000 accidents in the United States.

__T__ 3. About 45,000 people die every year in motor vehicle accidents.

__F__ 4. More accidents occur in September than any other month.

__T__ 5. More accidents occur on Friday than any other day.

__F__ 6. About 75% of all drivers wear seatbelts.

C. Key Words

Ask your teacher about any new words below. Listen to the sentences and fill in the correct words.

witness	crashed
intersection	hurt
damage	fault

1. The _damage_ to my car was over $3,000.
2. My sister _hurt_ her neck in the car accident.
3. The accident was his _fault_ . He went through a stop sign.
4. There are a lot of accidents at the _intersection_ of Pine Street and Mountain Avenue.
5. The car went off the street and _crashed_ into a tree.
6. The _witness_ saw the accident and gave the information to the police.

🔊 **D. First Listening**

Listen to the story of this car accident one or more times. On the diagram on page 80, show the accident scene right before the accident.

Where was Kim? Draw this car.

Where was the sports car? Draw this car.

Where was the witness? Put an **X** .

🔊 **E. Listen and Choose**

Read this information about the accident, then listen to the story again. Put a check in front of each statement that describes the accident.

____ 1. It was about 6:00 A.M.

____ 2. Kim was driving to work.

____ 3. The traffic was heavy.

____ 4. The sports car came from a side street.

____ 5. The sports car went through the red light.

____ 6. The sports car hit the front of Kim's car.

____ 7. Kim was hurt.

____ 8. Kim's car had a lot of damage.

____ 9. Kim drove her car home.

____ 10. A police officer saw the accident.

🔊 **F. The Police Report**

Listen to the story again. When the police arrived, they spoke to three people. Decide who they spoke to first, second, and third. Write *1st*, *2nd*, or *3rd* in the box under each picture.

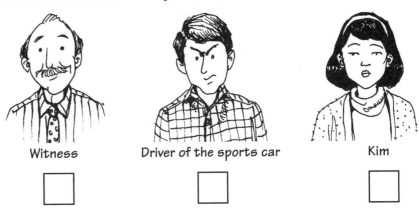

Witness   Driver of the sports car   Kim

- *past tense*
- *stress*

STRUCTURE

🔲 A. Listen and Write

Listen to these sentences. Write the past tense verb you hear.

1. _____was_____   6. _____
2. _____   7. _____
3. _____   8. _____
4. _____   9. _____
5. _____   10. _____

PRONUNCIATION

🔲 A. Same or Different

Listen to these two verbs. Decide if they are the same or different. Circle *same* or *different*.

1. same   different   6. same   different
2. same   different   7. same   different
3. same   different   8. same   different
4. same   different   9. same   different
5. same   different   10. same   different

🔲 B. Listen for Stress

Mark the word that is the loudest.

1. Her story is correct.
2. This man passed the red light.
3. She had the green light.
4. He had the red light.
5. I had the green light.
6. You had the red light.
7. He said she passed the red light.
8. He didn't hit my side.
9. He hit the other side.
10. The accident was his fault.

CONVERSATIONS

🔲 A. Match

Officer Clark made out reports on two accidents yesterday. Listen to these conversations between Officer Clark and the drivers. After each conversation, write the number of the correct driver.

CONVERSATION 1: Driver _____   CONVERSATION 3: Driver _____

CONVERSATION 2: Driver _____   CONVERSATION 4: Driver _____

🔲 B. Comprehension Questions

1. Listen to Conversations 1 and 2 again, then answer these questions.
   a. Do the two drivers agree about all the facts in this accident?
   b. Who is at fault in this accident?

2. Listen to Conversations 3 and 4 again, then answer these questions.
   a. Do the two drivers agree about how the accident happened?
   b. Who is at fault in this accident?

🔲 C. Repeating or Questioning

Listen to these short conversations between a driver and a police officer. In some sentences, the officer is repeating the information. In some sentences, the officer is questioning the information. He isn't sure that it is correct. Listen to these examples:

◢ **Example A:**   DRIVER: **I was driving along First Street.**
                   OFFICER: **You were driving along First Street.**

In Example A, the officer is repeating the information.

◢ **Example B:**   DRIVER: **I was driving along First Street.**
                   OFFICER: **You were driving along First Street?**

In Example B, the officer is questioning the information.
The intonation is the same as for a question.

Circle *repeating* or *questioning*.

1. repeating   questioning   6. repeating   questioning

2. repeating   questioning   7. repeating   questioning

3. repeating   questioning   8. repeating   questioning

4. repeating   questioning   9. repeating   questioning

5. repeating   questioning   10. repeating   questioning

🔲 D. Past Yes/No Questions

Listen carefully to each question. Write the first two words.

1. _____ _____ pass the red light?
2. _____ _____ tell the truth?
3. _____ _____ see the accident?
4. _____ _____ talk to the police?
5. _____ _____ hit her car?
6. _____ _____ go to the hospital?
7. _____ _____ have your license with you?
8. _____ _____ stop?
9. _____ _____ call an ambulance?
10. _____ _____ have a lot of damage?

INTERACTION

Sit in a small group. Be sure that one student in each group was in an accident or was a witness to an accident. The student will describe the accident in detail: the location of the accident, the traffic signals, the direction the vehicles were traveling, etc. The other students will draw a diagram of the accident. They will ask the questions below and complete the information.

Diagram:

Questions:

1. What time did the accident happen? _____
2. What were the weather conditions? _____
3. How fast were you going? _____
4. Who else was in the car? _____
5. Was anyone hurt? _____
6. What was the damage to your car? _____
7. Did the police come? _____
8. Whose fault was the accident? _____
9. What did you do after the accident? _____

MY NEIGHBOR

COMPREHENSION

A. Discuss

Talk about these questions.

Do you know your neighbors?
Do the people in your neighborhood ever help each other?

B. Before You Listen

This man was walking down Fourth Street on his way to visit a friend. What do you think happened to him? Who is going to help him?

C. Key Words

Ask your teacher about any new words below. Listen to the sentences and fill in the correct words.

neighborhood	alley
beat	mugged
acted like	passed

1. The man __Mugged__ an old woman and ran away with her purse.
2. The thief __beat__ the store owner, then stole the money.
3. The __alley__ between the buildings is dark and dirty.
4. When I was driving, an ambulance __passed__ me.
5. My __neighborhood__ is noisy and busy.
6. I am upset. When I saw my friend yesterday, she __acted like__ she didn't know me.

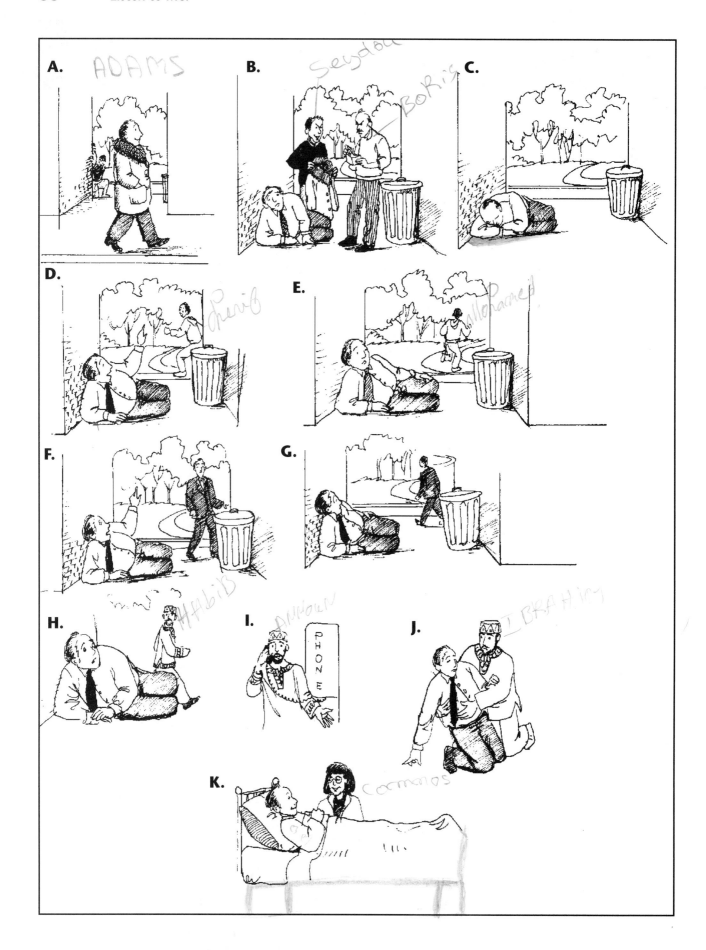

▢ D. First Listening

Look at the pictures on page 86 and listen to this story about a mugging as many times as you want. After you listen, tell the class any information you remember about the story. Answer these questions:

1. What happened to this man?
2. How many men passed the alley?
3. Who helped him?

▢ E. Listen and Write the Letter

Listen to these sentences. Write the letter of the correct picture.

1. _I_   6. _C_
2. _F_   7. _A_
3. _H_   8. _E_
4. _B_   9. _J_
5. _K_   10. _G_

▢ F. Listen and Choose

In this story, the speaker tells about the three men who saw him in the alley. Read these sentences, then listen to the story again. Which man is the speaker talking about? Write *1st*, *2nd*, or *3rd*.

_2_   1. He went to the same church.
_3_   2. He dressed differently.
_3_   3. He called the police.
_1_   4. He said, "I'll be right back."
_3_   5. He felt sorry for me.
_2_   6. He acted like he didn't see me.
_1_   7. He was from my neighborhood.
_3_   8. He stayed with me.

▢ G. Comprehension Questions

Listen and circle the correct answer.

1. a. to work   b. to church   c. to visit a friend
2. a. a man from his   b. two men   c. a friend
   church
3. a. in the morning   b. in the evening   c. at night
4. a. his coat and money   b. They mugged him.   c. in an alley
5. a. in the park   b. in an alley   c. in the church
6. a. a few minutes   b. an hour   c. all day
7. a. the first man   b. the second man   c. the third man

> • *past tense*
> • *pronunciation of* ed

STRUCTURE

🔲 A. Listen and Write

Listen to these sentences. Write the past tense verb you hear.

1. _____jumped_____
2. _____mussed_____
3. _____passed_____
4. _____shoulded_____
5. _____turned_____

6. _____helped_____
7. _____stopped_____
8. _____called_____
9. _____stayed_____
10. _____waited_____

PRONUNCIATION

🔲 A. Same or Different

You will hear two verbs. Decide if they are the same or different. Circle *same* or *different*.

1. same   different
2. same   different
3. same   different
4. same   different
5. same   different

6. same   different
7. same   different
8. same   different
9. same   different
10. same   different

🔲 B. *ed* Endings

Listen to the pronunciation of these verbs.

/d/	/t/	/Id/
played	walked	rented
turned	missed	needed

Look at the verbs below. Listen to the pronunciation of *ed*. Circle the pronunciation you hear.

1. waited   /d/ /t/ /Id/
2. called   /d/ /t/ /Id/
3. stopped   /d/ /t/ /Id/
4. acted   /d/ /t/ /Id/
5. stayed   /d/ /t/ /Id/

6. died   /d/ /t/ /Id/
7. passed   /d/ /t/ /Id/
8. helped   /d/ /t/ /Id/
9. shouted   /d/ /t/ /Id/
10. dressed   /d/ /t/ /Id/

CONVERSATIONS

🖭 A. Match

Listen to these conversations between a police dispatcher and four different callers. Number each picture.

🖭 B. Same or Different

Read each sentence. Then listen to the sentence on the tape. Decide if the meaning of the two sentences is the same or different. Circle *same* or *different*.

1. My car isn't here.	same	different
2. Come here fast.	same	different
3. Stay on the phone.	same	different
4. She wants to get into the car.	same	different
5. Someone is getting into my neighbor's house.	same	different
6. They are shouting out the window to a friend.	same	different
7. There's a problem in the apartment downstairs.	same	different

C. The Robbery

You are a clerk in a jewelry store. A few minutes ago a woman came into the store and asked to look at some expensive necklaces. Suddenly, she pulled out a gun, took the jewelry, and asked for the money in the cash register. Now, a police officer is asking you questions. Circle the correct answer.

1. a. She had a gun.

   b. She left very fast.

   c. She took about $5,000 in jewelry and cash.

2. a. About 15 minutes ago.

   b. For about five minutes.

   c. About $2,000 in cash.

3. a. No, no one was with her.

   b. No, no one else was in the store.

   c. No, she wasn't.

4. a. She was a tall, heavy woman with blond hair.

   b. She had a big pocketbook.

   c. She was nervous.

5. a. A small, black gun.

   b. She put everything in her pocketbook.

   c. A red dress.

6. a. Yes, it is.

   b. Yes, she was.

   c. Yes, she did.

7. a. No, no one else was in the store.

   b. Don't move!

   c. She stayed here about five minutes.

8. a. I was very surprised.

   b. She ran up the street.

   c. She was wearing big gold earrings.

9. a. No, she didn't get into a car.

   b. She ran up Main Street.

   c. She said, "Thank you" when she left the store.

INTERACTION

Imagine that you looked out the window of your home and saw the crime below. You called the police and reported the crime. Now, the police are interviewing you. They need information about the mugger. Sit with a partner and write an interview. One of you is the witness; the other is the police officer. Act out your conversation in front of the class.

WITNESS: _____

OFFICER: _____

WITNESS: _____

OFFICER: _____

WITNESS: _____

OFFICER: _____

WITNESS: _____

OFFICER: _____

WITNESS: _____

TAPESCRIPTS

UNIT 1: Ali

COMPREHENSION (pages 1–3)

C. Key Words Listen to the sentences and fill in the correct words.

1. My sister and I are both 24. We're twins.
2. I have a lot of relatives in the United States.
3. I visit my aunt and uncle about once a month.
4. George is single. He isn't married.
5. My father retired when he was 65 years old.
6. The couple who lives under us is very friendly.

Story

My name is Ali. I'm from Egypt. I'm a student at Oakdale University. I live with my aunt and uncle. We live in a small apartment building. There are four families in this building.

There's a family of four living under us, the Ramirez family. They're from Mexico. Mr. Ramirez is a letter carrier. Mrs. Ramirez is a telephone operator. They have two boys — they're twins, Manuel and Michael. They're ten years old and in the fourth grade.

Next to us, there's a single man. He's from India. Mr. Patel is old; I think he's about 68 years old. He's a retired teacher. He has a lot of relatives, and they visit him a lot.

In the fourth apartment, there's a young couple from Vietnam, Cao and Linh Tran. Cao's a student at Oakdale University. We're in the same English class and we walk to school together. Linh is an x-ray technician.

All the people in my apartment building are friendly. They're good neighbors.

F. Listen for Numbers Look at the picture and answer these questions with the correct number.

1. How many people live in Ali's apartment?
2. How many apartments are there in this building?
3. How many children do Mr. and Mrs. Ramirez have?
4. How old are the boys?
5. How many people live in the apartment next to Ali?
6. How old is Mr. Patel?
7. How many people live on the first floor?
8. How many people live in this apartment building?

G. Comprehension Questions Listen and circle the correct answer.

1. Where is Ali from?
2. Who does he live with?
3. Where does the Ramirez family live?
4. Is Mr. Ramirez a letter carrier or a telephone operator?
5. Where is Mr. Patel from?
6. Is he married?
7. Are Ali and Cao in the same English class?

STRUCTURE (page 4)

A. Listen and Write Listen to these sentences. Write the verb you hear: *am*, *is*, or *are*.

1. My name is Ali.
2. I'm from Egypt.
3. They're from Mexico.
4. Mrs. Ramirez is a telephone operator.
5. He's from India.
6. Cao is a student at Oakdale.
7. We're in the same English class.
8. Linh is an x-ray technician.
9. All the people in my apartment building are friendly.
10. They're good neighbors.

PRONUNCIATION (pages 4–5)

A. The Article *A* All of these sentences have the article *a*. Listen carefully and put the article in the correct place in the sentence.

Example: He's a retired teacher.

1. He's a letter carrier.
2. Cao's a student.
3. There's a family living under us.
4. She's a telephone operator.
5. I'm a student at Oakdale University.
6. We live in a small apartment building.
7. She works in a hospital.
8. Mr. Patel is a single man.
9. He has a lot of relatives.
10. Cao and Linh are a young couple from Vietnam.

CONVERSATIONS (pages 5–6)

Conversation 1:

CAO: Who is it?
ALI: It's me, Ali. Let's go!
CAO: Let's go?
ALI: Come on. We're late.
CAO: No, we're not. Remember, there's no English class today. The teacher has a meeting.
ALI: Oh! That's right! I forgot.
CAO: Come on in. Have a cup of coffee. The next class is an hour from now.
ALI: OK. Sounds good.

Conversation 2:

MR. PATEL: Hi, there.
MRS. RAMIREZ: Hi. How's everything?
MR. PATEL: Good, good. I'm waiting for my brother.
MRS. RAMIREZ: Your older brother? The one from Arcadia?
MR. PATEL: Yes. He's coming at 3:00. How're your boys?

MRS. RAMIREZ: Busy. Michael's on the soccer team and
                 Manuel's on the swimming team.
MR. PATEL: Those boys love sports. Well, say hello to
                 the family.
MRS. RAMIREZ: I will. Have a nice day.

Conversation 3:
MICHAEL: Hi, Mrs. Tran.
MRS. TRAN: Hi. How's your soccer team?
MICHAEL: Good.
MRS. TRAN: When's your first game?
MICHAEL: Tomorrow, in the park.
MRS. TRAN: Maybe I can watch you some afternoon.
MICHAEL: OK. The games always start at 4:00. Bye.
MRS. TRAN: Bye.

C. How   Listen to these questions. Circle *How's* or
How're.

1. How's school?
2. How're the boys?
3. How're you?
4. How's everything?
5. How's the weather?
6. How're your aunt and uncle?
7. How're your neighbors?
8. How's the family?
9. How's the soccer team?
10. How're your classes?

D. Hello and Good-bye   Listen to these expressions.
Some you can use when you say *Hello*. Some you can use
when you say *Good-bye*. Circle *Hello* or *Good-bye*.

1. How's everything?
2. How are you?
3. So long.
4. Have a nice day.
5. Good morning.
6. What's new?
7. Take care.
8. Good talking with you.
9. See you.
10. Hi!

UNIT 2: Back in School

COMPREHENSION (pages 7–9)

C. Key Words   Listen to the sentences and fill in the
correct words.

1. Our coffee break is 15 minutes.
2. I feel nervous when I speak English.
3. This is my second year in the United States.
4. For homework, we have to do pages 14 and 15.
5. We talk to each other before class.
6. I'm going to the cafeteria for a cup of coffee.

Story

It's September 10th, the second week of school. This
is the Dallas Adult School. There are classes for math,
reading, and typing. And there are classes for English.

My class is in room 201. I'm in beginning English, the
first class. This is my fourth year in the United States, but I
don't speak English. I only know some easy words, like
"girl" and "car" and "house."

I'm a little nervous about school. Maybe I'm too old to
learn English. I'm 40 years old. English is difficult for me.

But, I want to learn English very much. This year my
three children are in school. They all speak English.
Sometimes, they speak English to each other, and I don't
understand them. I want to talk to their friends and I want
to talk to their teachers.

There are ten students in our class. Six are like me,
they're from Mexico. Sonia, my sister, is in my class.
There are three students from Vietnam and one from
India.

Our teacher is Ms. Lang. She's young, only about 23 or
24. But she's a good teacher. I understand her because she
speaks slowly. We all speak English in class.

Our class is three hours every day. It's from 9:00 to
12:00. There's a break at 10:30. We all go to the cafeteria
and talk and drink coffee.

I like school. It's not easy and we have a lot of
homework. But I'm happy to be back in school.

G. True or False   Listen to these statements. Circle *T* if
the statement is true, *F* if the statement is false.

1. This is the first day of school.
2. Ana knows a lot of words in English.
3. Ana is nervous about school.
4. English is easy for her.
5. Her children speak English.
6. The class is small.
7. All of the students are from Mexico.
8. The teacher is a young man.
9. At the break, the students do their homework.
10. She is happy she is back in school.

STRUCTURE (page 10)

A. Listen and Write   Listen to these sentences. Circle
the words you hear: *there is, there are,* or *they're*.

1. There's a cafeteria in our school.
2. They're from Vietnam.
3. There are six students from Mexico.
4. There are classes for math.
5. They're happy to be in school.
6. There's a break at 10:30.
7. There are classes for ESL.
8. They're older now.

PRONUNCIATION (page 10)

A. Listen for Negatives Listen carefully for *is* or *isn't*. Circle the word you hear.

1. My class is in room 201.
2. It isn't the first week of school.
3. My sister is in my class.
4. My brother isn't in my class.
5. English isn't easy for me.
6. Our teacher isn't old.
7. She's 23 years old.
8. She isn't from India.
9. Our class is three hours a day.
10. The break is at 10:30.

ANNOUNCEMENTS (page 11)

Announcement 1:
We are going to use the book *Beginning English* in this class. You need to buy this book. *Beginning English* is $20. You can buy it any day this week in the main office.

Announcement 2:
Class is from 9:00 to 12:00. We have a 15 minute break at 10:30. The break is from 10:30 to 10:45. You can sit in class, or walk around, or go to the cafeteria. But, please, be back in class on time. I start teaching again at 10:45. I don't want you to walk in late when everyone is working.

Announcement 3:
If you park in the school parking lot, you need a parking sticker. A sticker is $5.00. You put it on the window of your car. Then you can park in the school parking lot. You can get your sticker in the main office.

Announcement 4:
Please do not bring your children to class for any reason. If your child is sick, do not bring him to class. If your child has a day off from school, please find a baby-sitter or ask a friend to watch the child.

Announcement 5:
English class is on Monday, Wednesday, and Friday mornings. There are other classes on Tuesday and Thursday. Math and typing are at the same time. They're on Tuesday and Thursday from 9:00 to 11:00. If you want to register for math or typing, go to the main office.

Announcement 6:
If you are absent, call the main office. Give your name and say you are in English 1. Tell the secretary that you cannot come to class. The secretary will give me the information. When you come back to class, talk to me about your class work. I will give you all the papers from class.

C. Excuse Me The students are asking Ms. Lang to repeat some information. Listen and complete these conversations.

1. MS. LANG: You can buy the book in the main office.
   STUDENT: Excuse me. Where?
2. MS. LANG: The book is $20.
   STUDENT: Excuse me. How much?
3. MS. LANG: Class begins at 9:00.
   STUDENT: Excuse me. What time?
4. MS. LANG: The break is at 10:30.
   STUDENT: Excuse me. What time?
5. MS. LANG: The break is 15 minutes.
   STUDENT: Excuse me. How long?
6. MS. LANG: You can get the sticker in the main office.
   STUDENT: Excuse me. Where?
7. MS. LANG: A parking sticker is $5.00.
   STUDENT: Excuse me. How much?

UNIT 3: City or Country

COMPREHENSION (pages 13–15)

C. Key Words Listen to the sentences and fill in the correct words.

1. I don't smoke because I don't want to get cancer.
2. When a child is sick, a parent takes care of him.
3. Can you help me choose a good doctor?
4. When my sister graduated from nursing school, she received three job offers.
5. A 300-bed hospital has room for three hundred patients.
6. A general hospital takes care of all kinds of patients— people with heart problems, people with cancer, and people who were in car accidents.

Story
   Gloria is a student in nursing school. She's going to graduate next month. She has two job offers. One is in a city hospital, the other is in a country hospital.
   The hospital in the city is large; it's a 600-bed hospital. It's a cancer hospital. It gives excellent care to its patients. It's in a big city, near museums, theaters, and restaurants. The salary is high, $34,000 a year. But apartment rents are high, too.
   The hospital in the country is small; it's a 50-bed hospital. It's a general hospital. It takes care of all kinds of patients. It's in a beautiful area, near lakes, rivers, and mountains. The salary is average, $27,000 a year. But apartment rents are low.
   Gloria likes the city and the country. She doesn't know which hospital to choose.

F. Listen and Write the Letter Listen to these sentences. Write in the letter of the correct picture.
1. The salary is average.
2. Apartment rents are low.
3. Gloria is a student in nursing school.
4. This hospital takes care of all kinds of patients.
5. It's near museums, theaters, and restaurants.

6. Apartment rents are high.
7. It's near lakes, rivers, and mountains.
8. This hospital only takes care of cancer patients.

G. Comprehension Questions Listen and circle the correct answer.

1. What is Gloria?
2. Is she working now?
3. How large is the hospital in the city?
4. Where is the cancer hospital?
5. What kind of hospital is the country hospital?
6. What's the salary at the country hospital?
7. Which job offer will Gloria take?

STRUCTURE (page 16)

A. Listen and Write Listen to these sentences about the story. Write the verb you hear: *is* or *are*.

1. Gloria is a student in nursing school.
2. The hospital in the city is large.
3. It's a cancer hospital.
4. Apartment rents are high.
5. There are many restaurants in the city.
6. The other hospital is in the country.
7. There are 50 beds in the hospital.
8. The salary is average.
9. Apartment rents are low.
10. Both job offers are good.

PRONUNCIATION (page 16)

A. Singular or Plural Listen to these sentences. Decide if the noun is singular or plural. Circle the word you hear.

1. Gloria is a student.
2. She has two job offers.
3. The hospital in the city is large.
4. It takes care of cancer patients.
5. The hospital is near museums.
6. Gloria likes the country.
7. It's near beautiful lakes.
8. The salary is average.
9. Apartment rents are low.
10. She doesn't know which hospital to choose.

CONVERSATIONS (page 17)

Conversation 1:
GLORIA: I looked at a lot of apartments.
FATHER: What's the rent in the city?
GLORIA: A small one-bedroom is about $700.
FATHER: And in the country?
GLORIA: A large one-bedroom is about $400.

Conversation 2:
FATHER: What about a car?
GLORIA: Well, I don't need a car in the city.
FATHER: You can walk or take the bus.

GLORIA: But I have to have a car in the country.
FATHER: A good used car is about $7,000. And then you'll need insurance and gas.

Conversation 3:
FATHER: What are the hours at City Hospital?
GLORIA: They want me to work the night shift, from 11:00 to 7:00 A.M.
FATHER: And at General Hospital?
GLORIA: They need nurses on all shifts. I can work day, or evening, or night.
FATHER: Which shift do you want?
GLORIA: The day shift, from 7:00 to 3:00.

Conversation 4:
FATHER: Is the vacation the same?
GLORIA: At City Hospital, it's two weeks the first year. The second year, it's three weeks.
FATHER: And at General Hospital?
GLORIA: It's three weeks the first year and three weeks the second year.

Conversation 5:
FATHER: What about the job?
GLORIA: Well, at City Hospital, I'll be a regular nurse. And I'll only work with cancer patients.
FATHER: Hmm. City Hospital is the best cancer hospital in this state.
GLORIA: And at General Hospital, they need nurses in the emergency room.
FATHER: Is that what you want? The emergency room?
GLORIA: I think so. It sounds more interesting.

B. How About? To ask or find out more information, we often use *How about* or *What about*. Write the sentences you hear.

1. How about the salary?
2. What about the rent?
3. How about vacation time?
4. What about the job?
5. What about the area?

UNIT 4: A Bus Ride

COMPREHENSION (pages 19–21)

C. Key Words Listen to the sentences and fill in the correct words.

1. The bus was so crowded that I couldn't find a seat.
2. His seeing-eye dog helps him cross the street safely.
3. Please turn that music down. It's too loud.
4. The young boy offered the woman his seat.
5. Many blind people wear dark glasses.
6. My boss gets angry when I'm late for work.

Story

Debbie lives about five miles from school. She always drives. Today her car is at the garage for new brakes, so she's taking the bus. At this moment, Debbie's getting on the bus. She needs exact change. She has five quarters, but she needs one more. She's looking for another quarter in her bag.

The bus is crowded and noisy. There's no place to sit and a lot of people are standing. One boy is listening to his radio. The music is very loud.

Mrs. Wu got on the bus before Debbie. She's holding onto a pole and using her cane. She's looking for a seat. Michael is getting up and offering Mrs. Wu his seat. She's smiling and thanking him.

Kathy is smoking a cigarette. When she's nervous, Kathy starts to smoke. She's late for work and the bus isn't moving. She's thinking about her boss. When someone is late, she gets angry. Kathy is sitting next to Joanne. Joanne hates cigarette smoke. She's pointing to the No Smoking sign and asking Kathy to put out her cigarette.

Kevin is sitting on the bus with his seeing-eye dog, Jet. Jet is lying quietly next to Kevin's seat. Kevin is blind, but Jet gets him to and from work with no problems. Kevin is trying to listen to the bus driver because he always calls out the names of the bus stops. He can't hear because the music is so loud.

Finally, the bus is moving. Debbie doesn't want to take the bus again this afternoon. At school, she's going to ask her friend for a ride home.

F. Who Questions Answer these *Who* questions about the story. Write the name of the person on the line.

1. Who is looking for a seat?
2. Who is smoking?
3. Who is looking for a quarter?
4. Who is trying to listen to the names of the stops?
5. Who is offering Mrs. Wu his seat?
6. Who is asking Kathy to stop smoking?

G. Comprehension Questions Listen and circle the correct answer.

1. Why is Debbie taking the bus?
2. How much is the bus fare?
3. Is Debbie going to sit or stand on the bus?
4. Why is Kathy nervous?
5. What sign is Joanne pointing to?
6. Why is Kevin listening carefully?
7. How is Debbie going to get home?

STRUCTURE (page 22)

A. Listen and Write Listen to these sentences. Write the present continuous verb you hear.

1. Debbie is taking the bus to school.
2. She's looking for another quarter.
3. Mrs. Wu is using her cane.
4. Michael is offering Mrs. Wu his seat.

5. She's thanking him.
6. Kathy is smoking a cigarette.
7. She's sitting next to Joanne.
8. Kathy is thinking about her boss.
9. Kevin is trying to listen to the bus driver.
10. His dog is lying next to him.

PRONUNCIATION (page 22)

A. His or Her Listen to these sentences. Circle *his* or *her*.

1. A boy is listening to his radio.
2. Debbie always drives her car to work.
3. Her car is at the garage.
4. She's looking in her bag.
5. Michael is offering his seat to Mrs. Wu.
6. She's on her way to a doctor's appointment.
7. She's using her cane.
8. Kevin is sitting with his dog.
9. He's on his way to work.
10. Debbie is going to ask her friend for a ride home.

CONVERSATIONS (page 23)

Conversation 1:

WOMAN 1: Excuse me. There's no smoking on this bus.
WOMAN 2: No smoking?
WOMAN 1: That's right. See the sign?
WOMAN 2: That's crazy. I can't smoke anywhere.
WOMAN 1: Well, you can't smoke on this bus.

Conversation 2:

MAN: How much is the fare?
DRIVER: A dollar fifty.
MAN: Here's $2.00.
DRIVER: Sorry, sir. Exact change only.
MAN: But I don't have exact change.
DRIVER: Sorry. There's nothing I can do.

Conversation 3:

MAN: Hey, my wallet! Where's my wallet?
DRIVER: Are you sure you had your wallet?
MAN: Of course. I had it when I paid my fare. Someone on this bus took my wallet.
DRIVER: Maybe you dropped it?
MAN: No, I put it in my pocket after I paid you.

Conversation 4:

BOY: Ma'am. Here, take my seat.
WOMAN: Oh. Thank you so much. You are very polite.
BOY: That's OK.

Conversation 5:

BOY: Sir, how do you cross the street?
MAN: Jet, here, helps me. When the light is red for the cars, he walks into the street and I go with him. When the light is green, he just stands there and I stand and I wait with him.
BOY: Wow, he's really a smart dog.
MAN: Yes, he is.

Conversation 6:

WOMAN 1: I had to take the bus to school today.
WOMAN 2: Where's your car?
WOMAN 1: At the garage. It needs new brakes.
WOMAN 2: Look, I leave about 4:00. Do you need a ride?
WOMAN 1: I'd love a ride.
WOMAN 2: Okay. I'll meet you at the library at 4:00.
WOMAN 1: Great! At the library at 4:00. Thanks.

B. Place and Time When we plan to meet a person, we often repeat the place and time to be sure we have the correct information. Listen to each statement. Fill in the exact place and time.

1. I'll meet you at the library at 4:00.
2. I'll see you in the cafeteria at 2:00.
3. I'll pick you up at the bus stop at 9:00.
4. I'll see you by the front door at 1:30.
5. I'll meet you in Room 24 at 10:00.
6. I'll be at your house at 7:30.
7. I'll pick you up on the corner at 6:30.
8. I'll meet you at the restaurant at 12:00.
9. I'll be at your office at 1:30.
10. I'll meet you at the book store at 3:30.

C. Offering Help In each conversation below, one person is offering help. Decide if the second person's answer means "Yes, thank you." or "No, thanks." Circle *Yes* or *No*.

1. A: Do you need a ride home?
   B: I'd love a ride home.
2. A: Here's a seat.
   B: Thank you very much.
3. A: Do you need a pencil?
   B: Thanks, I have one.
4. A: Here's a dictionary.
   B: That's OK. I have one in my backpack.
5. A: Do you want a cup of coffee?
   B: Thanks.
6: A: Here's a pencil.
   B: Thank you.
7. A: Do you need some help?
   B: Thanks, but George is going to help me.
8. A: Do you need a quarter?
   B: Thanks, but I have one.
9. A: Do you want a soda?
   B: I'd love a soda.
10. A: Here's a calculator.
    B: Thank you.

UNIT 5: The Supermarket

COMPREHENSION (pages 25–27)

C. Key Words Listen to these sentences and fill in the correct words.

1. When he was running, the boy knocked over some boxes of cookies.
2. When I go to the supermarket, my youngest child sits in the cart.
3. He's buying a large bunch of grapes.
4. Where's the spaghetti? It's in aisle five.
5. My children are adding more food to my cart.
6. She's angry because her children are running around the store.

Story

Oh, no! Here comes Mrs. Ryan with her four children. Every Friday night it's the same story. The supermarket manager is watching them from the service counter, his hand on his head.

Mrs. Ryan is smiling and pushing her cart up and down the aisles. Kelly, the youngest, is sitting in the cart and screaming. Mrs. Ryan isn't listening. She's at the meat counter, picking out some chicken. Kelly is crying louder and louder. She wants ice cream.

Marc is helping his mother. He's putting food in the cart when she isn't looking. He's adding cookies, potato chips, and doughnuts.

The supermarket manager is talking to Tessa. He's telling her she can't eat the bananas. He's taking a bunch of grapes from her, too.

One of the employees is walking toward the manager. She's angry; she's pulling a child with her. When he was running, Jeff knocked over five bottles of soda. Another employee is mopping the floor.

Thank goodness, Mrs. Ryan is finished. She's walking out of the store, pushing her cart. Her children are following quietly behind her.

"Good-bye." Mrs. Ryan is smiling at the manager. "We'll see you next week."

F. Listen and Write the Letter Listen to these sentences. Write the letter of the correct picture.

1. Kelly is sitting in the cart and screaming.
2. Marc is putting some food in the cart.
3. Mrs. Ryan is walking out of the store.
4. An employee is mopping the floor.
5. One of the employees is taking Jeff to the manager.
6. Here comes Mrs. Ryan with her four children.
7. The supermarket manager is taking a bunch of grapes from Tessa.
8. Mrs. Ryan is saying, "We'll see you next week."

G. Comprehension Questions Circle the correct answer.

1. When does Mrs. Ryan go food shopping?
2. Where is Kelly?
3. Why is Kelly crying?
4. Is Marc really helping his mother?
5. What is Tessa doing?
6. What is the employee mopping up?
7. Why is the manager happy?

STRUCTURE (page 28)

A. Listen and Write Listen to these sentences. Write the present continuous verb you hear.

1. Mrs. Ryan and her children are walking into the supermarket.
2. The manager is watching them.
3. Mrs. Ryan is pushing a cart.
4. She's picking out some chicken.
5. Marc is putting food in the cart.
6. He's adding cookies and doughnuts.
7. Tessa is eating a banana.
8. He's taking the grapes from her.
9. He's talking to her.
10. The children are following their mother out of the store.

PRONUNCIATION (page 28)

A. Listen for Negatives Listen to these sentences. Circle the verb you hear.

1. The store manager isn't smiling.
2. Marc is putting food in the cart.
3. Mrs. Ryan isn't looking at him.
4. Kelly is screaming.
5. Mrs. Ryan isn't listening to her.
6. She isn't watching her children.
7. Jeff isn't pushing the cart.
8. The produce manager isn't eating a banana.
9. He's talking to Tessa.
10. Mrs. Ryan is walking out of the store.

ANNOUNCEMENTS (page 29)

A. Prices Write the correct price. You will hear each price two times.

1. 79¢
2. $2.99
3. 69¢
4. $1.49
5. 84¢
6. $3.29
7. $1.25 a lb
8. 99¢ a lb.
9. 3 for $1.00
10. 2 for $3.00

B. Supermarket Announcements Listen to these sale announcements. Find the item and write the sale price.

Attention, Shoppers. Thank you for shopping at FoodTown.

Please check out the savings in our meat department. We have whole chickens on sale this week. Our grade A chickens are now only 69¢ a pound. That's right, shoppers, only 69¢ a pound.

Shoppers, you save more at FoodTown. Your family will enjoy the specials in our bakery department. This week, our doughnuts are only 25¢ each. Buy some today for breakfast tomorrow. And bring home one of our fresh-baked pies. We have apple, cherry, and blueberry. Large pies are on sale for $5.99, small pies are only $3.99.

Shoppers, our manufacturers are offering you savings plus this week. Try Premium spaghetti. This week, you can buy two boxes of spaghetti for only a dollar. It's easy to find Premium. It's the spaghetti in the bright yellow box.

All Clear detergent is cutting their already low prices. All Clear is that super detergent for your really dirty wash. A large container is only $2.69 this week.

And Chunky Soups has a special offer for you. Their thick, rich soups are great for lunch, dinner, or an after-school snack. Every can of Chunky Soup is just 89¢ a can.

C. Smart Shoppers Paul and Susan are at the supermarket. They are checking prices to find the cheapest brand. Listen to their conversations, then circle the one they will buy.

1. SUSAN: Lucky Peanut Butter is $1.99 a pound.
   PAUL: Tasty is a little less, it's $1.89 a pound.
2. SUSAN: Mrs. K's Italian dressing is $1.80.
   PAUL: Aunt Ida's Italian dressing is $1.90.
3. SUSAN: FoodTown Rice is $2.29 for five pounds.
   PAUL: I can't believe the difference in price. Solo Rice is $3.99 for five pounds.
4. SUSAN: Crispy Flakes are $2.59 a box.
   PAUL: Fruit Flakes are $2.49 a box and they taste better.
5. SUSAN: Pride Tomato Sauce is $1.89 a jar.
   PAUL: Tillie's Tomato Sauce is $1.79 a jar.
6. SUSAN: Tasty Yogurt is on sale. Two for a dollar.
   PAUL: But look at Andy's Yogurt. It's 49¢ a container.
7. SUSAN: FoodTown Bread is $1.14.
   PAUL: Best Bread is $1.40.

UNIT 6: The Disco

COMPREHENSION (pages 31–33)

C. Key Words Listen to the sentences and fill in the correct words.

1. That man is a good dancer. His partner is a great dancer!
2. I can't hear you! The music is too loud.
3. I like many kinds of music, but my favorite is rock 'n roll.
4. He's not talking with his girlfriend. He's talking with someone else.
5. When the song is over, let's sit down.
6. She met a nice man at the disco last week.

Story

It's Saturday night and Olga is at her favorite disco, the Music Box.

Olga is standing at the bar with her friend, Sonia. Many people are at the bar, eating and talking. Olga isn't eating and she isn't talking with her friend. She's looking at the dance floor. She knows a lot of the people, but she's looking for someone special.

Last Saturday, Olga was at the same disco. She met a nice man. He asked her to dance and they danced for an hour. Then Olga had to leave. Is he here tonight? Is he looking for her? What's his name?

The band is playing a loud song. Almost everyone is dancing. Then, she sees him. He's dancing with someone else. Who is she? Is she his girlfriend? Oh, well. Olga is going to talk to her friends and have a good time. She's going to forget about him.

The song is over. His partner is walking away! He's looking around, then he sees Olga. The band is beginning the next song and he's walking toward her. He's asking her to dance. They walk onto the dance floor together. Olga is smiling and he is, too.

F. Listen and Write the Letter
Listen to these sentences. Write the letter of the correct picture.

1. He's dancing with someone else.
2. His partner is walking away!
3. Olga met a nice man last Saturday night.
4. Olga is standing at the bar.
5. He's walking toward her.
6. Olga is looking for someone special.
7. Olga is dancing with him.
8. He's asking Olga to dance.

G. Comprehension Questions
Listen and circle the correct answer.

1. Is this Olga's first time at the Music Box?
2. Where is Olga standing?
3. Who is she looking for?
4. When did she meet him?
5. Does she know the young man's name?
6. What is the young man doing?
7. At the end of the story, where is Olga?

STRUCTURE (page 34)

A. Listen and Write Listen to these sentences. Write the verb you hear. Some sentences are negative.

1. Olga and her friend are standing at the bar.
2. Olga isn't eating.
3. She's looking at the dance floor.
4. She isn't talking with Sonia.
5. Many people are dancing.
6. Olga isn't dancing.
7. Olga isn't having a good time.
8. His partner is walking away.
9. He's asking her to dance.
10. They're smiling.

PRONUNCIATION (page 34)

A. Statement or Question Listen to these sentences about the story. Decide if each is a question or a statement. Circle *statement* or *question*.

1. Olga is at the disco.
2. Is Olga at the disco?
3. Is she dancing?
4. She's at the bar.
5. Is he here tonight?
6. He's here.
7. Is he looking for her?
8. He's looking at her.
9. He's dancing.
10. Is she his girlfriend?

CONVERSATIONS (page 35)

Conversation 1:
FEMALE 1: There he is. The guy with the glasses.
FEMALE 2: Glasses and long hair?
FEMALE 1: No, he's got short hair. And he's wearing a tie.
FEMALE 2: He's good-looking.
FEMALE 1: Yeah, he is.

Conversation 2:
FEMALE 1: That's him. The man I met last week.
FEMALE 2: Which one?
FEMALE 1: He's got short black hair. And he's wearing blue jeans and a striped shirt.
FEMALE 2: I see him. He's dancing with the girl with blond hair.
FEMALE 1: Yeah, that's him.

Conversation 3:
FEMALE 1: That's the man I was telling you about.
FEMALE 2: Where?
FEMALE 1: Over there, at the bar. He's got short black hair and a moustache.

FEMALE 2: And he's eating a pizza?
FEMALE 1: Yes.
FEMALE 2: He's cute.
FEMALE 1: Yeah, he is.

Conversation 4:
FEMALE 1: I see him. He's over there, near the band.
FEMALE 2: Which one?
FEMALE 1: He's got short, curly hair.
FEMALE 2: Is he wearing glasses?
FEMALE 1: No, it's the other guy. He's talking to the man with glasses.

B. Which One? Listen to these short phrases or sentences. Match each with the correct man. Write the number of the statement in the boxes under the correct picture.

1. He's got long hair.
2. The man with the earring.
3. He's bald.
4. The man with the glasses.
5. He's wearing a striped shirt.
6. He's got short, curly hair.
7. He's wearing a jacket and tie.
8. The man with the beard.
9. He's wearing a sweater.
10. He has a moustache.

C. Agree Agree with each statement you hear. Circle the correct response.

1. She's friendly.
2. It's hot in here.
3. He's a good singer.
4. She's nice.
5. This pizza is good.
6. He's talkative.
7. This place is noisy.
8. She's a good dancer.
9. He's cute.
10. She's pretty.

UNIT 7: Vacation

COMPREHENSION (pages 37–39)

C. Key Words Listen to the sentences and fill in the correct words.

1. We don't need gas. The tank is full.
2. Four people can sleep in our camper.
3. Remember to pack your sunglasses and a hat.
4. We're going directly to Dallas; we're not going to stop anywhere.
5. They're going to hike in the mountains.
6. In Florida, the ocean is warm. In California, it's cold.

Story

Everything is ready for our vacation. The gas tank is full. The camper is packed. We're going to leave tomorrow morning.

This is the first year that my wife and I have two weeks for vacation. We live in Columbus, Ohio. It's a big city. Our children were born here. They think that everyone lives in a city. They have never been in the country. They have never seen the ocean.

We're going to drive to Florida, but not directly. First, we're going to drive east, to the Shenandoah National Park in Virginia. It's about 400 miles from here. We're going to stay there for two days. We're going to hike one day and rent mountain bikes the next day. Maybe we will see some deer or bears. After that, we're going to drive another 400 miles to Wilmington, North Carolina. My sister lives there. We're going to stay with her and her family for three days. She lives about a mile from the ocean. We're going to swim, have picnic lunches, and walk along the beach. The kids are going to collect shells. Then, it's about 600 miles from there to Orlando, Florida. We have a reservation at a park about two miles from Disney World. We're going to visit Disney World and Epcot and Universal Studios. If we have time, we're going to watch a show at Sea World. By Friday, everyone is going to be tired. We're going to pack the camper and start back to Ohio. If we drive back north, it's about 1,000 miles. We're not going to stop anywhere special, we're just going to drive nine hours a day for two days. On Sunday, we're going to unpack and relax.

F. Comprehension Questions Listen and circle the correct answer.

1. Where does this family live?
2. When are they going to go on vacation?
3. Where are they going to sleep?
4. Did they take a two-week vacation last summer?
5. Is this the first time that the children will visit their aunt in North Carolina?
6. Are they going to drive home directly?
7. How long will it take them to drive from Florida to Ohio?

STRUCTURE (page 40)

A. Listen and Write Listen to these sentences. Write the future verb you hear. In conversational English, *going to* sometimes sounds like *gonna*.

1. We're going to leave tomorrow.
2. We're going to drive to Florida.
3. We're going to stay there for two days.
4. The family is going to hike.
5. We're going to swim in the ocean.
6. The children are going to collect shells.
7. We're going to visit Disney World.
8. Everyone is going to be tired.
9. We're going to unpack.
10. Everyone is going to relax.

PRONUNCIATION (page 40)

A. For or From Listen to these sentences. Circle the preposition you hear.

1. Everything is ready for our vacation.
2. We borrowed the camper from my brother.
3. We saved $2,000 for this trip.
4. We have film for the camera.
5. We have two weeks for vacation.
6. The park is about 400 miles from here.
7. We're going to stay there for two days.
8. We're going to stay with my sister for three days.
9. She lives about a mile from the beach.
10. It's about 1,000 miles from here to there.

B. Question Words Listen to these questions about vacations. Write the question word or words.

1. Where are you going to go?
2. When are you going to leave?
3. What are you going to do there?
4. Who are you going to visit?
5. How long are you going to stay?
6. When is she going to leave?
7. Where is she going to stay?
8. How much money is she going to take?
9. When is her plane going to leave?
10. Who is she going to go with?

CONVERSATIONS (page 41)

Conversation 1:
A: Are you going to go anywhere special on your week off?
B: Yes, I'm going to visit my sister in Santa Fe.
A: Santa Fe?
B: Hmm-hmm. In New Mexico. I'm going to fly down there on Sunday.
A: What's there to do in Santa Fe?
B: Oh, it's beautiful there. It's in the mountains. There are lots of art museums and stores with Indian jewelry and great little restaurants with Mexican food. I love it there.

Conversation 2:
A: Sumira, are you going to spend the summer in the United States?
B: No, this summer I'm going back to Japan.
A: That's great! When was the last time you saw your family?
B: Two years ago.
A: Wow, that's a long time. See you in September.

Conversation 3:
A: So, what're you going to do this summer?
B: I'm going to be right here.
A: Here? At school?
B: Yeah.
A: How come?
B: I failed biology. I have to take it again this summer.

Conversation 4:
A: When are you going to leave?
B: Tonight.
A: Tonight?
B: Yes. After work. We're going to drive straight to Washington.
A: That's a good idea. You'll be there on Saturday morning.
B: We're going to the Smithsonian Museum on Saturday. And on Sunday, we're going to take the kids to the zoo.
A: You'll be tired for work on Monday.
B: I know.

Conversation 5:
A: So, what are your summer plans?
B: I don't know.
A: Do you have a job?
B: Nope.
A: Are you going to take any courses?
B: Uh-uh.
A: Are you going to take a vacation?
B: I don't think so.
A: Well, have a good summer.

Conversation 6:
A: I called a real estate agent.
B: Good idea.
A: And we have a house. In July.
B: Where is it?
A: In Oceanside. About a block from the beach.
B: How long are you going to rent it for?
A: For two weeks. Two weeks of sun and sand and water.
B: Sounds great.

B. Yes or No In conversational English, many words and sounds mean yes or no. Listen to the examples. Then, listen to these questions and answers. Decide if the answer means yes or no. Circle yes or no.

Yes	No
Yeah	Nope
Yup	Nah
Uh-huh	Uh-uh
Hmm-hmm	No way

1. A: Are you going to go on vacation?
   B: Yeah.
2. A: Are you ready?
   B: Yup.
3. A: Are you packed?
   B: Uh-huh.
4. A: Are you going to work this summer?
   B: Uh-uh.
5. A: Are you going to take any courses?
   B: No way.
6. A: Are you going to take any time off?
   B: Nah.
7. A: Are you going to visit your family?
   B: Uh-huh.

8. A: Are you going to drive there?
   B: Hmm-hmm.
9. A: Are you going to go to Europe again this summer?
   B: Nope.
10. A: Are you going to work at the pool again?
    B: Uh-uh.

C. Repeating In conversation, the listener often repeats the last word or phrase of the speaker, using question intonation. This shows the listener is interested or surprised and would like more information.

Example 1: A: **I'm going to visit my sister in Santa Fe.**
            B: **Santa Fe?**
Example 2: A: **I'm going to be right here.**
            B: **Here?**

Listen to each speaker's summer plans. Then write the last word or phrase you hear.

1. I'm going back to Japan.
2. I'm going to get a job in Alaska.
3. I'm going to teach tennis.
4. I'm going to leave tomorrow.
5. I'm going to spend the summer in China.
6. I'm going to get married.
7. I'm going to get my pilot's license.
8. I'm going to learn how to speak Russian.
9. I'm going to work on a fishing boat.
10. I'm going to drive a taxi.

UNIT 8: Eduardo

COMPREHENSION (pages 43–45)

C. Key Words Listen to the sentences and fill in the correct words.

1. I live alone in a small apartment.
2. He's packing his clothes and the presents he's bringing.
3. At first, he didn't speak any English.
4. Sometimes when I think of my family, I feel lonely.
5. He's getting serious about a girl from his native country.
6. They're going to go to the beach together.

Story

Eduardo is looking at his airline ticket again and smiling. Tomorrow he's going to be with his family in Cartagena. He's going to leave the snow and cold of New Jersey for the hot sun of his native Colombia.

Eduardo left Colombia about three years ago. At first, he lived with a cousin in Trenton. Now, he rents a small apartment with a friend. He goes to school and he works six or seven days a week. He has a big TV, a car, and nice clothes. But he's lonely, very lonely.

Eduardo is packing his suitcase. He's looking at a picture of Yolanda. Yolanda and he went to the same high school together in Colombia and their parents are good friends. They've been writing for two years. At first, they wrote as friends. But now, their letters are more serious.

They have plans for this vacation. They're going to walk on the beach together, go to parties, and visit Yolanda's family. How is he going to feel about her? How is she going to feel about him? Eduardo is going to return to the United States in one month. He's thinking, "Am I going to return alone? Or, are we going to return together as husband and wife?"

E. Listen and Write the Letter Listen to these sentences. Write the letter of the correct picture.

1. Eduardo is packing his suitcase.
2. They're going to walk along the beach together.
3. Eduardo is looking at his ticket.
4. They've been writing letters for two years.
5. He works six or seven days a week.
6. They're going to visit Yolanda's family.
7. He's going to leave the snow and cold of New Jersey.
8. Eduardo lives with a friend.

G. Comprehension Questions Listen and circle the correct answer.

1. What time of the year is it in the United States?
2. Where does Eduardo live?
3. Who does he live with?
4. Why does he feel lonely?
5. When was the last time Eduardo saw his family?
6. How long is he going to stay in Colombia?
7. How does Eduardo know Yolanda?

STRUCTURE (pages 46)

A. Listen and Write Listen to these sentences. Write the future tense verb you hear.

1. Eduardo is going to leave tomorrow.
2. He's going to fly to Colombia.
3. He's going to stay in Colombia for one month.
4. He's going to see his family and friends.
5. They've going to be happy to see him.
6. He's going to tell them about his life in the United States.
7. He's going to see Yolanda.
8. They're going to talk about the future.
9. They're going to visit her family.
10. Eduardo is going to return to New Jersey next month.

PRONUNCIATION (page 46)

A. *Her / His / Him* Listen to these sentences. Complete them with *her*, *his*, or *him*. Note that the *h* is often silent.

1. He's packing his suitcase.
2. He's going to visit his family.
3. He's looking at her picture.
4. He's going to see her tomorrow.
5. She's going to be happy to see him.
6. He's going to talk to her about the future.
7. She's going to take him to a family party.
8. He's going to buy her a ring.
9. He's going to ask her to marry him.
10. She's going to go back to the United States with him.

CONVERSATIONS (page 47)

Conversation 1:

EDUARDO: And Yolanda, you don't speak English.

YOLANDA: Yes, I'm worried about that. My friend told me that English is very difficult.

EDUARDO: I'm not home a lot. I work nine or ten hours a day.

YOLANDA: What am I going to do all day?

EDUARDO: You'll feel lonely, too. You'll miss your family.

YOLANDA: Eduardo, I can't leave Colombia. Can you move back here?

Conversation 2:

EDUARDO: And Yolanda, you don't speak English.

YOLANDA: I know. I can go to school.

EDUARDO: I'm not home a lot. I work nine or ten hours a day.

YOLANDA: Maybe I can find a job.

EDUARDO: You'll feel lonely, too. You'll miss your family.

YOLANDA: Eduardo, you are going to be my family. I know it isn't going to be easy, but we can do it together.

Conversation 3:

EDUARDO: And Yolanda, you don't speak English.

YOLANDA: I know. Is English difficult?

EDUARDO: No, but it isn't easy. And I'm not home a lot. I work nine or ten hours a day.

YOLANDA: Well, I can read and watch TV and write letters.

EDUARDO: You'll feel lonely, too. You'll miss your family.

YOLANDA: Eduardo, I'm not sure I can leave my family. My aunt and uncle live in New Jersey. I think I'll visit them and see how I like the United States.

B. *Can / Can't* Listen to these sentences. Complete them with *can* or *can't* and the verb.

1. I can go to school.
2. I can't leave Colombia.
3. I can find a job.
4. I can't move back to Colombia.
5. I can't speak English.
6. I can write letters.
7. I can visit my aunt and uncle.

C. Interested? Two people are discussing plans for the next week. The first person is making a suggestion. Decide if the second person is interested or not. Check *Interested* or *Not Interested*.

1. A: My sister is having a party tomorrow night.
   B: Sounds great.
2. A: There's a big dance at school next week.
   B: Let's go. I really liked the disc jockey last time.
3. A: Tom and Diane called. They invited us for dinner on Saturday night.
   B: I don't know. All they talk about is their kids.

4. A: I can get tickets for the baseball game tomorrow.
   B: You can? And it's supposed to be a great game!
5. A: My aunt and uncle invited us for dinner next week.
   B: Maybe another time.
6. A: That new movie is starting at the theater downtown this weekend.
   B: Let's wait. Maybe next week.
7. A: Let's go out for dinner.
   B: I always like to go out for dinner!

UNIT 9: Divorce

COMPREHENSION (pages 49–51)

C. Key Words Listen to the sentences and fill in the correct words.

1. My sister and her husband argue about money, the car, the children, everything.
2. They don't love each other anymore.
3. Their parents are living far away in another state.
4. You can call me anytime, I'll always have time to talk to you.
5. My sister lives near me in the same town.
6. We're going on vacation together in the summer.

Story

Marsha and Tom Gibson are sitting at the kitchen table. Tom is nervous and upset, and he's smoking. Marsha's eyes are red. She looks tired. Their two sons are eight and ten and they're sitting with them. Tony and George know that their parents are having problems. They argue all the time. They don't talk to each other anymore. Their mom and dad aren't happy together anymore. Now, their parents are telling the boys that they're going to get a divorce.

Their mother is talking first. She's telling them that she loves them and their father loves them, too. But, she and their father are having problems. They aren't going to live together as a family anymore. It has nothing to do with the boys. The boys are going to live with her. They're going to stay in the same house, go to the same school, and be with all their friends.

Now, their father is talking. He's going to leave the house this weekend. He's not going to move far away; he's going to be in the next town. Two weekends a month, the boys are going to stay with him. And, they're going to be with him one month in the summertime. He'll take his vacation then, and they'll go to the beach. The boys can call him anytime. He's going to be near. It'll be better this way.

Tony and George don't really understand what's happening. They know that their parents aren't happy. But, they want everyone to stay together.

E. Listen and Write the Letter   Listen to these sentences. Write the letter of the correct picture.

1. The boys can call their father anytime.
2. Tom and Marsha are going to get a divorce.
3. Two weekends a month, the boys are going to stay with their father.
4. Tom is smoking.
5. They're going to stay in the same house.
6. Tony and George don't really understand what's happening.
7. They'll go to the beach in the summertime.
8. Tom is going to leave the house this weekend.

G. Comprehension Questions   Listen and circle the correct answer.

1. What do Tom and Marsha argue about?
2. How old are the boys?
3. What school are the boys going to go to?
4. When is their father going to leave?
5. Where is he going to move?
6. When can the boys call their father?
7. How often will the boys see their father?

STRUCTURE (page 52)

A. Listen and Write   Listen to these sentences. Write the future tense verb you hear. In spoken English, *going to* sounds like *gonna*.

1. Tom and Marsha are going to get a divorce.
2. The boys are going to live with their mother.
3. They're going to stay in the same house.
4. They're going to go to the same school.
5. They're going to be with all their friends.
6. They aren't going to live together anymore.
7. Their father is going to leave this weekend.
8. He's going to move to the next town.
9. The boys are going to stay with him two weekends a month.
10. He's going to be near.

B. Listen for Tense   Listen to these sentences. Decide if the verb is about right now or the future. Circle *right now* or *future*.

1. They are sitting at the kitchen table.
2. Tom is smoking.
3. Tom and Marsha are having problems.
4. They're going to get a divorce.
5. They're talking to the boys.
6. The boys are going to live with their mother.
7. They're going to see their father two weekends a month.
8. The boys are looking at their parents.
9. They're asking questions.
10. It's going to be difficult for everyone.

C. Time Expressions   Listen to these sentences. Fill in the time expression.

1. The boys are going to see their father two weekends a month.
2. They can call him anytime.
3. They're going to go on vacation one month in the summer.
4. Tom and Marsha argue all the time.
5. Tom is going to leave this weekend.
6. He's going to move in a few days.
7. The boys are going to see their father next weekend.
8. They're going to call their father on Sunday night.
9. Marsha is going to talk to a lawyer next week.
10. The boys are going to go to the same school next year.

CONVERSATIONS (pages 53–54)

Conversation 1:
WOMAN: When are you going to fix the shower?
MAN: Tomorrow.
WOMAN: Tomorrow. Everything is tomorrow. You never do anything around the house.
MAN: I'm tired.
WOMAN: You always say that. You do nothing. You just sit in front of the TV all day.

Conversation 2:
WOMAN: Larry, how much was this camera?
MAN: Two hundred dollars.
WOMAN: Two hundred dollars! We don't have two hundred dollars for a camera. How are we going to pay the rent tomorrow?
MAN: I don't know. You bought a new coat last week. That was two hundred fifty dollars.
WOMAN: Well, I needed a coat.
MAN: And I needed a camera.

Conversation 3:
Man: Where's Gina?
WOMAN: She's out with her friends.
MAN: Where?
WOMAN: At Lisa's house. They're just watching TV and talking.
MAN: When's she going to be home?
WOMAN: At 11:00.
MAN: 11:00? 11:00 is too late for a 16-year-old.
WOMAN: 11:00 is not too late for a 16-year-old.
MAN: I don't want her out this late.
WOMAN: This isn't late. It's Saturday night and she's just at another girl's house.

Conversation 4:
WOMAN: Sorry I'm late.
MAN: Late? Sue, you're an hour late!
WOMAN: Well, I met a friend and we started to talk.
MAN: You knew I needed the car.
WOMAN: You're just visiting your brother. He can wait.

MAN: I'm taking him to the dentist. I told you I needed the car at 11:00.

WOMAN: Look, I said I was sorry.

MAN: You never think about me. It's always what you want.

B. Listen for Stress The most important word or words in a sentence are stressed. These words are the loudest and strongest in the sentence. Listen and circle the word or words that are stressed.

Example: You never do anything.

1. You always say that.
2. You do nothing.
3. You just sit in front of the TV.
4. You're no help at all.
5. I do everything.
6. You're an hour late.
7. I needed a coat.
8. And I needed a camera.
9. You never think about me.
10. It's always what you want.

UNIT 10: Ana and Peter

COMPREHENSION (pages 55–57)

C. Key Words Listen to the sentences and fill in the correct words.

1. Flight 963 is going to land at 4:46.
2. When my wife is away on business, I miss her.
3. I spend time with my children in the evening.
4. She isn't home yet; she's still at work.
5. In the afternoon, I put my youngest child in bed for a nap.
6. The shuttle between New York and Boston leaves every hour.

Story

Ana gets up at 5:15 A.M. four mornings a week. She showers, dresses, and eats breakfast. She leaves her husband and children, who are still sleeping, by 6:00 A.M. Ana is an airline pilot and she flies the daily shuttle from New York to Boston. Her husband, Peter, is a househusband. He stays home with the children, ages two, six, and eight.

Peter likes staying home. He says that most fathers don't spend enough time with their children. He enjoys his family. But, it's a lot of work. In the morning, he cleans, shops, and does the laundry. In the afternoon, when the youngest child takes a nap, he fixes TVs. He has a small business at home. When the children come home from school, they take bike rides or play outside. Then the

children do their homework or play while Peter makes dinner.

Ana is usually home by 6:00 P.M. After dinner, she plays with the children and reads to them. When they're in bed, Peter and Ana have some time for themselves.

But some days Ana doesn't get home until late. On those days, she doesn't see the children. Tonight, it's eight o'clock and Ana is still in Boston. She's calling Peter. The weather is bad and the flight is going to be late. Peter is telling her not to worry. The children can see her tomorrow. Peter misses Ana when she isn't home at night. But, he also knows how much she likes her job. He'll stay up and wait for her.

E. Listen and Write the Letter Listen to these sentences. Write the letter of the correct picture.

1. Peter cleans the house.
2. They take bike rides.
3. Peter and Ana have some time to themselves.
4. The children do their homework.
5. He fixes TVs.
6. She reads to the children.
7. Ana is an airline pilot.
8. The weather is bad and the flight is going to be late.

G. Comprehension Questions Listen and circle the correct answer.

1. About what time does Ana start work?
2. Who takes care of the children?
3. Does Peter like staying home?
4. What does Peter do in the afternoon?
5. When does Ana see the children?
6. When do Ana and Peter spend time together?
7. Why is Ana calling Peter?

STRUCTURE (page 58)

A. Listen and Write Listen to these sentences. Write the present tense verb you hear.

1. Ana gets up at 5:15 A.M.
2. She eats breakfast.
3. The children sleep until 7:00.
4. Peter stays home.
5. He enjoys his family.
6. He has a small business at home.
7. They take bike rides.
8. After dinner, she reads to the children.
9. Some days Ana doesn't get home until late.
10. Peter misses Ana at night.

PRONUNCIATION (page 58)

A. Same or Different You will hear two verbs. Decide if they are the same or different. Circle *same* or *different*.

1. shower   showers
2. flies   fly

3. leave   leave
4. play   play
5. takes   take
6. play   plays
7. reads   reads
8. have   have
9. doesn't see   don't see
10. like   likes

B. Pronunciation of *s* Listen to the pronunciation of these verbs.

/s/	/z/	/ɪz/
eats	says	dresses
likes	cleans	fixes

Look at the verbs below. Listen to the pronunciation of *s*. Circle the pronunciation you hear.

1. takes
2. has
3. enjoys
4. looks
5. misses
6. reads
7. relaxes
8. shops
9. watches
10. stays

CONVERSATIONS (pages 59–60)

Conversation 1:

LISA: Dad, what's for dinner?
DAD: Lasagna.
LISA: Good. I love lasagna.
TOM: Dad, I don't like lasagna.
DAD: Well, you'll love my lasagna. OK, kids, I need some help. Lisa, you start to make the salad. Tom, you set the table. Mom's going to be home in a few minutes.

Conversation 2:

LISA: Dad, can we go for a bike ride?
TOM: Yeah!
DAD: OK. Where do you want to go?
TOM: Can we go to the park?
LISA: No, I want to go to the ice cream store.
DAD: Today, it's the park. Go get your helmets.

Conversation 3:

DAD: Tom, do you have a book out from the library?
TOM: I don't know.
DAD: Well, here's a note from the library. It says you have a book overdue. It's *All About Airplanes*.
TOM: Oh, that's right. It's in my room.
DAD: Go and get it. We can all walk to the library.

Conversation 4:

DAD: Do you have any homework?
TOM: I don't have any.
LISA: I have math homework.
DAD: OK, Lisa, you sit at the kitchen table and start your homework. Tom, you can read or play with Brian.
TOM: Can I watch TV?
DAD: You know that you can't watch TV on school nights.

B. *Like / Don't like* Listen to these short conversations. Give your opinion. Complete *one* of each pair of sentences. Don't worry about spelling.

Example: A: **What's for lunch?**
              B: **Pizza.**

1. A: What kind of pizza did you order?
    B: Pepperoni.
2. A: What's for dinner?
    B: Fish.
3. A: What color sweater did you buy?
    B: Blue.
4. A: What kind of cookies did you make?
    B: Chocolate chip.
5. A: Who's the lead actor?
    B: Bill Murray.
6. A: Which CD did you buy?
    B: Michael Jackson.
7. A: Who's playing?
    B: The Yankees.
8. A: Where are we going?
    B: To the beach.
9. A: What flavor ice cream did you buy?
    B: Coffee.
10. A: What did you get for dessert?
    B: Apple pie.

C. Short Answers Listen carefully for *he* or *she* in these questions. Circle the correct answer.

1. Does he cook dinner?
2. Does he like lasagna?
3. Does she help her father?
4. Does she wear a helmet?
5. Does he have the library book?
6. Does she want to go to the park?
7. Does he like to read?
8. Does he have any homework?
9. Does she sometimes come home late?
10. Does he watch TV at night?

UNIT 11: Volunteers

COMPREHENSION (pages 61–63)

C. Key Words Listen to the sentences and fill in the correct words.

1. Sometimes it is difficult for older people to prepare a meal for themselves.
2. A soccer team has 11 players.
3. The Recreation Department in our town has many sports programs for children.
4. Infants need a lot of love and attention.
5. If a mother is an alcoholic, her baby often has physical problems.
6. The coach wants the boys to practice more.

Story

Over 50 percent of Americans give a few hours a week to help in their communities, their churches, or in their children's schools. These people are volunteers.

Walter volunteers for "Meals on Wheels." On Tuesdays, he delivers hot meals. At 11:30 on Tuesday morning, he drives to a church hall and picks up the meals. He drives to 11 homes in his town. Most of the people live alone, but there are a few couples. Many of the people are older, most are over 80. They can't cook because they have physical problems, such as back or leg or heart problems. Walter says hello and talks for a few minutes. It takes Walter about two hours to deliver the meals.

Tom is a soccer coach. His ten-year-old son loves soccer. The Recreation Department in town has a sports program. The fathers and mothers are the coaches. During the soccer season, each team practices one afternoon a week in the late afternoon. On Saturday, the teams play one another. Tom likes the exercise, the excitement, and the special time with his son.

Kate volunteers at Children's Hospital one afternoon a week. Kate works in the Infant Care Unit. Some of the children have AIDS. Some of the children have mothers who are alcoholics or drug users. The babies need lots of love and attention. Kate is a cuddler. She holds the babies, feeds them, talks to them, and sings to them. Kate says, "I give them love, but they give me more love in return."

E. Listen and Decide
Listen to these sentences about the volunteers in the story. Circle *Walter*, *Tom*, or *Kate*.

1. This person has a ten-year-old son.
2. This person drives a car when he volunteers.
3. This person only volunteers part of the year.
4. This person enjoys talking.
5. This person volunteers in a hospital.
6. This person likes sports.
7. This person enjoys babies.
8. This person volunteers at lunch time.

F. Comprehension Questions
Listen and circle the correct answer.

1. How many Americans volunteer?
2. When does Walter deliver the meals?
3. Why can't the people cook?
4. Who is on Tom's soccer team?
5. When are the soccer games?
6. Why are the children in the hospital?
7. Is Kate sick?

STRUCTURE (page 64)

A. Listen and Write Listen to these sentences. Write the present tense verb you hear.

1. Over 50 percent of Americans volunteer a few hours a week.
2. Walter volunteers for "Meals on Wheels."
3. He picks up the meals at a church hall.
4. Many of the people have physical problems.
5. It takes Walter about two hours.
6. The Recreation Department has a sports program.
7. Some of the children have alcoholic mothers.
8. The babies need lots of love and attention.
9. Kate sings to them.
10. They give me more love in return.

PRONUNCIATION (pages 64–65)

A. Of (All of, Most of, Many of, Some of, A few of, None of) Listen and complete these sentences. The word *of* is often reduced. We do not say or hear the *f*. Listen to this example.

Example: Some of the volunteers work in the morning.

1. Many of the people are older.
2. Some of the children have AIDS.
3. All of the volunteers enjoy their work.
4. Most of the people live alone.
5. All of the people have physical problems.
6. None of the volunteers get paid.
7. A few of the volunteers work in the evening.
8. All of the children need love.
9. Some of the mothers are alcoholics.
10. None of the teams play on Sunday.

CONVERSATIONS (pages 65–66)

Conversation 1:

INTERVIEWER: Do you volunteer?
MALE: Well, I'm in the choir at my church.
INTERVIEWER: Oh, you sing.
MALE: Yes, we practice on Wednesday night from eight to ten, and then I sing at the nine o'clock service on Sunday morning.

Conversation 2:

INTERVIEWER: You're on the Rescue Squad, aren't you?
FEMALE: Yes, I give time on Monday night. I volunteer from eight to twelve.

INTERVIEWER: How many calls do you get on a typical night?
FEMALE: Sometimes, it's real quiet and we just sit and talk. But at other times, it's real busy. Like last Monday night, there were two accidents and one heart attack.

Conversation 3:
INTERVIEWER: Do you volunteer?
FEMALE: Yes, I work at my daughter's school one morning a week, usually on Monday.
INTERVIEWER: What do you do?
FEMALE: I work in the library. I put the books away. Sometimes, I sit and read with a child.

Conversation 4:
INTERVIEWER: Do you volunteer any time?
MALE: No, I don't have any time now. But when I have more time, I'd like to give an hour or two.

Conversation 5:
INTERVIEWER: Do you volunteer?
MALE: Yes, there's a soup kitchen near my house. I work there on Saturday morning. I make sandwiches or I cut up vegetables, things like that.
INTERVIEWER: Who comes to the soup kitchen?
MALE: All kinds of people. Some of them are unemployed. Some of them are alcoholics. All of them are having a hard time now. I like to talk to them. They tell me about their plans and hopes for the future.

Conversation 6:
FEMALE: I volunteer at a nursing home.
INTERVIEWER: A nursing home? With old people?
FEMALE: Well, I really like older people. I remember my grandmother.
INTERVIEWER: What do you do there?
Female: Well, I know it sounds crazy, but I do the ladies' fingernails.
INTERVIEWER: Their fingernails?
FEMALE: Sure. I file them and put nail polish on them. The ladies love it. And they talk to me about their children and their grandchildren. They're really interesting.
INTERVIEWER: When do you go?
FEMALE: On Friday afternoon, after school.

C. Listen for Prepositions Listen to these sentences from the story. Complete them with the correct preposition.
1. He sings in the choir at church.
2. They meet on Wednesday.
3. They practice from 8:00 to 10:00.
4. He sings at the 9:00 service.
5. She gives time on Monday night.

6. She volunteers from 8:00 to 12:00 .
7. She works at her daughter's school in the library.
8. He works at a soup kitchen near his house.
9. She volunteers at a nursing home.
10. She goes there on Friday afternoons.

UNIT 12: Good Health

COMPREHENSION (pages 67–69)

C. Key Words Listen to the sentences and fill in the correct words.
1. My father turned 50 on his last birthday.
2. When he had his heart attack, the man collapsed on the floor.
3. Many hospitals have cardiac units to care for patients with heart problems.
4. No one in my family smokes, except me.
5. You can walk one mile the first month. The second month, you can increase that to two miles.
6. When it's very hot in a room, I sometimes feel dizzy.

Story

Len just turned 50 last week. He's a successful businessman, the president of a large company. Len lives in a beautiful home with his wife and two daughters. He drives an expensive car and wears the best clothes. He has everything that money can buy, except for one thing, good health.

It happened one afternoon at the office. Len didn't feel well all that morning. He was hot and a little dizzy. He remembers the terrible pain in his chest as he collapsed. For two weeks Len was in the cardiac care unit of the hospital. Before leaving the hospital, Len got his orders from the doctor. He's trying to follow them.

Len has to lose weight and exercise each day. He used to smoke a pack of cigarettes every day. He can't smoke anymore. In the morning, Len has to walk one mile. He can't have his usual bacon and eggs for breakfast. And he has to drink decaffeinated coffee. For lunch, he can't order the salty french fries that he loves so much. For dinner, he has to eat fish or chicken and a vegetable. Len hates vegetables and he dreams about steak.

Len also has to slow down at the office. At first, he can only work four hours a day. He can increase his hours each month, but he can't work more than seven hours a day. After work, he has to exercise at a health club. Len misses the long hours and the excitement of the office. How did this happen to him? He's only 50 years old.

E. Listen and Write the Letter Listen to these sentences. Write the letter of the correct picture.
1. Len can't smoke.
2. Len has to slow down at the office.
3. He drives an expensive car.
4. He had terrible pains in his chest.

5. For dinner, he has to eat fish or chicken.
6. He has to walk one mile before breakfast.
7. Len got his orders from the doctor.
8. He has to exercise at a health club.

G. Comprehension Questions Listen and circle the correct answer.

1. How old is Len?
2. What happened to him?
3. Why did he have a heart attack?
4. How long was he in the hospital?
5. What does he like to eat?
6. When does he exercise?
7. How many hours a day can he work now?

STRUCTURE (page 70)

A. Listen and Write Listen to these sentences. Write the present tense verb you hear.

1. Len is the president of a large company.
2. He has two daughters.
3. They live in a beautiful house.
4. He drives an expensive car.
5. He remembers the terrible pains in his chest.
6. He has to lose weight.
7. Len hates vegetables.
8. He likes salt on his food.
9. He dreams about steak.
10. He misses the long hours at the office.

B. Listen for Modals Listen to these sentences. Write the complete verb you hear. Listen for *has to, can,* or *can't.*

Examples: A: He has to watch his diet.
B: He can eat chicken and fish.
C: He can't eat steak.

1. He has to lose weight.
2. He can't drink regular coffee.
3. He has to drink decaf coffee.
4. He can't put salt on his food.
5. He has to exercise before and after work.
6. He has to join a health club.
7. He can't smoke anymore.
8. He can go back to work next month.
9. He has to slow down at the office.
10. He can't work ten hours a day anymore.

PRONUNCIATION (page 71)

C. Short Answers Listen to these questions about the story. Answer with *Yes, he can.* or *No, he can't.*

1. Can Len smoke?
2. Can Len eat sausage and eggs for breakfast?
3. Can he drink decaf coffee?
4. Can he drink regular coffee?
5. Can he put salt on his food?
6. Can he eat fish?
7. Can he eat steak?
8. Can he go back to work?

9. Can he increase his hours each month?
10. Can he work eight hours a day?

CONVERSATIONS (pages 71–72)

Conversation 1:
DOCTOR: Len, your blood pressure is still too high.
LEN: What is it?
DOCTOR: 150 over 90. I'm prescribing Dinatol. Take it twice a day, in the morning and in the evening.
LEN: OK.

Conversation 2:
DOCTOR: Are you smoking again?
LEN: Well, only five or six a day.
DOCTOR: Len, smoking is the number one factor in heart problems. You have to stop. Completely. You can't even have one cigarette a day.
LEN: I'll try.
DOCTOR: Len, you were lucky this time.

Conversation 3:
DOCTOR: How many hours a day are you working now?
LEN: Four hours.
DOCTOR: And how do you feel? Tired?
LEN: No, not at all. I'm ready to put in a full day.
DOCTOR: Try five hours this month. See how you feel.

Conversation 4:
LEN: Doctor, I need to talk to you about coffee.
DOCTOR: Coffee?
LEN: I hate decaf coffee. Decaf coffee is hot brown water.
DOCTOR: Len, you used to drink six or seven cups of coffee a day.
LEN: You don't understand. I need a real cup of coffee.
DOCTOR: OK, have one cup of regular coffee in the morning. But after that one cup, it's all decaf or nothing.

Conversation 5:
DOCTOR: Your weight is down again. You lost five more pounds.
LEN: Yeah, that's 15 pounds altogether.
DOCTOR: How far are you walking in the morning?
LEN: One mile. That takes me about 15 minutes.
DOCTOR: Good. You can increase that little by little to two miles.

Conversation 6:
DOCTOR: Your cholesterol level was 290. Now, it's 270. You need to bring that down to between 200 and 220.
LEN: I'm trying.
DOCTOR: Here's some information on which foods you can eat and which foods to stay away from.
LEN: Everything I like is no good for me.
DOCTOR: Well, Len, it's your heart.
LEN: OK, OK. I hear you.

C. Same or Different Read each sentence. Then, listen to the sentence on the tape. Decide if the meaning of the two sentences is the same or different. Circle *same* or *different*.

1. You can't even have one cigarette a day.
2. I'm ready to put in a full day.
3. Try five hours this month.
4. You used to drink six or seven cups of coffee a day.
5. A real cup of coffee.
6. Your weight is down again.
7. You can increase that little by little to two miles.
8. Your cholesterol level was 290. Now it's 270.
9. Stay away from food like steak and eggs.
10. I hear you.

D. The Doctor's Orders These are the doctor's orders. Check the sentence you hear.

1. Take this twice a day.
2. Take one tablet before each meal.
3. Take one tablet every four hours as needed for pain.
4. Take three tablets now, then one tablet three times a day.
5. Take one tablet one hour after each meal.
6. Take two teaspoonfuls before you go to bed.
7. Take a half teaspoonful three times a day.

UNIT 13: Fast Thinking

COMPREHENSION (pages 73–75)

C. Key Words Listen to the sentences and fill in the correct words.

1. Last night, there was a robbery at our friend's house.
2. The police arrested the man who stole my money.
3. He focused the camera to get a better picture of the children.
4. I jumped out of bed when I heard a loud scream.
5. Last week, I saw a woman who was stealing a sweater from a store.
6. This roll of film takes 24 pictures.

Story

Last month, the Wilsons went to Green Trees Park. Jim and Sally sat under the trees and talked and read. The children played ball. Sally decided to take a picture of the children. She took out her camera and walked over to them. She focused her camera. Then, she heard a scream. Sally looked up. A man was stealing a woman's purse. He was running in her direction.

Sally thought fast. She took three pictures of the man. When the police came, she gave them the film.

The next day, one of Sally's photographs was in the newspaper. Under the picture was the story of the robbery. In a few hours, the police knew the man's name and address. They went to his house and arrested him. The man is now serving three months in jail.

F. Listen and Write the Letter Listen to these sentences. Write the letter of the correct picture.

1. One of Sally's photographs was in the newspaper.
2. The Wilsons went to the park.
3. Sally took a picture of the man.
4. When the police came, Sally gave them the film.
5. She focused her camera.
6. Jim and Sally sat under the trees and talked and read.
7. A man was stealing a woman's purse.
8. The children played ball.
9. The man is now serving three months in jail.
10. The police arrested the man.

G. Listen and Decide You will hear a sentence from the story. Decide what happened after that. Circle the correct answer.

1. Sally and Jim sat under a tree.
2. Sally decided to take a picture of the children.
3. She heard a scream.
4. A man was running in her direction.
5. The police came.
6. The police learned the man's name and address.
7. The police went to the man's house.

STRUCTURE (pages 76)

A. Listen and Write Listen to these sentences. Write the past tense verb you hear.

1. Sally and Jim sat in the park.
2. They read their books under a tree.
3. Sally took her camera out of her purse.
4. She heard a woman scream.
5. Sally thought fast.
6. She took three pictures of the man.
7. The police came in a few minutes.
8. The next day, a photograph of the man was in the newspaper.
9. In a few hours, the police knew his name.
10. The police went to the man's house.

B. Tense Contrast Listen to these sentences. Decide the tense of the verb. Circle *present*, *past*, or *future*.

1. He goes to the park on Sunday.
2. He takes a lot of pictures of his children.
3. His wife gave him a new camera.
4. She also got him two rolls of film.
5. He's going to take pictures at his son's soccer game.
6. He sent some photographs to his mother.
7. His mother likes to get pictures of her grandchildren.
8. He's going to put the photos in an album.
9. He's going to buy a telephoto lens.
10. He went to the camera store.

PRONUNCIATION (page 76)

A. Listen and Circle You will hear two verbs. Decide if they are the same or different. Circle *same* or *different*.

1. come   came
2. took   take
3. stole   steal
4. ran   run
5. thought   thought
6. saw   saw
7. hear   heard
8. give   gave
9. knew   knew
10. drive   drove

CONVERSATIONS (pages 77–78)

Conversation 1
A: I can't believe it!
B: He was such a nice person.
A: Yeah. He always said, "Good morning."
B: But why? Why did he do it?
A: Who knows?

Conversation 2
A: You're not serious!
B: I am. John robbed a woman in the park.
A: You're kidding! Are they sure it was John?
B: They're sure. Some woman took his picture. Look at the front page.
A: That's John all right! Whoa!

Conversation 3:
A: Did you see this?
B: No.
A: Here, look at this picture.
B: That's John! What did he do?
A: He stole some woman's purse.
B: Really?
A: Yes, really. Read the story.

Conversation 4:
A: You're not going to believe this.
B: What?
A: The police were here about an hour ago.
B: The police?
A: They arrested John.
B: John List? The man who lives upstairs?
A: Yeah. They said he robbed a woman in the park yesterday.
B: That's hard to believe.

C. Question or Statement Listen to these sentences about the story. Decide if each is a question or a statement. Circle *statement* or *question*.

Examples: STATEMENT: John robbed a woman.
QUESTION: John robbed a woman?

1. John robbed a woman?
2. His picture's in the newspaper.
3. He stole her purse?
4. John's a nice guy.
5. Some woman took his picture.
6. The police came here.
7. They did?
8. They arrested him?
9. They arrested him today.
10. He's in jail?

D. Dictation Listen and write these questions.
1. What did he do?
2. Why did he do it?
3. What did he steal?
4. When did the police come?
5. Where did you hear about this?
6. What did the police do?

UNIT 14: The Accident

COMPREHENSION (pages 79–81)

C. Key Words Listen to the sentences and fill in the correct words.
1. The damage to my car was over $3,000.
2. My sister hurt her neck in the car accident.
3. The accident was his fault. He went through a stop sign.
4. There are a lot of accidents at the intersection of Pine Street and Mountain Avenue.
5. The car went off the street and crashed into a tree.
6. The witness saw the accident and gave the information to the police.

Story

Last night, Kim was driving home from work. She was on Broad Street. Traffic was heavy and she was driving carefully. At the intersection of Broad Street and Park Avenue, Kim had the green light and drove into the intersection. Suddenly, a sports car went through the red light and crashed into the side of Kim's car. No one was hurt, but the damage to Kim's car was heavy. She couldn't drive home.

The police arrived in two minutes. Kim explained the accident. She said she had the green light and the other driver went past the red light. But, she couldn't believe the other driver's story. He told the officer that the accident was Kim's fault. He said that Kim passed the red light! The officer looked at both drivers and asked, "Did anyone see the accident? Were there any witnesses?" A man was standing on the sidewalk. He walked over to the officer and said, "I was driving right in back of this woman. Her story is correct. This man went through the red light and hit the side of her car."

STRUCTURE (page 82)

A. Listen and Write Listen to these sentences. Write the past tense verb you hear.

1. Traffic was heavy.
2. Kim had the green light.
3. She drove into the intersection.
4. A small sports car went through the red light.
5. It crashed into the side of Kim's car.
6. The police arrived in two minutes.
7. Kim explained the accident.
8. The officer looked at both drivers.
9. A man walked over to the officer.
10. He hit the side of her car.

PRONUNCIATION (page 82)

A. Same or Different Listen to these two verbs. Decide if they are the same or different. Circle *same* or *different*.

1. pass   passed
2. crashed   crashed
3. ask   asked
4. say   said
5. had   had
6. explain   explained
7. looked   looked
8. arrive   arrived
9. walked   walked
10. happen   happened

B. Listen for Stress Mark the word that is the loudest.

1. Her story is correct.
2. This man went through the red light.
3. She had the green light.
4. He had the red light.
5. I had the green light.
6. You had the red light.
7. He said she passed the red light.
8. He didn't hit my side.
9. He hit the other side.
10. The accident was his fault.

CONVERSATIONS (pages 83–84)

Conversation 1:

OFFICER: OK, let me get the facts.
DRIVER: Well, I was driving along First Street.
OFFICER: OK, you were driving along First Street.
DRIVER: And that woman just backed out of her driveway, right into the street. She didn't stop at the end of her driveway and check to see if anyone was coming.
OFFICER: She didn't stop and check?
DRIVER: No, she just came right into the street. And I hit her.

Conversation 2:

OFFICER: OK, let me hear your story.
DRIVER: Well, I was backing out of my driveway. And I stopped at the end to see if anyone was coming.
OFFICER: You stopped at the end of your driveway?
DRIVER: Yes. I always stop at the end. And I didn't see anyone.
OFFICER: You didn't see anyone?
DRIVER: No. And I backed into the street and this man hit me.

Conversation 3:

OFFICER: I'm filling out the police report. So, you were driving along Bay Avenue.
DRIVER: Yes. I was driving along Bay, in back of that minivan. And suddenly, he stopped real fast. I couldn't stop in time. It was hard to see him because he didn't have any taillights.
OFFICER: He didn't have any taillights?
DRIVER: No, he didn't.
OFFICER: OK. Let me check on that.

Conversation 4:

OFFICER: I need some information for the accident report.
DRIVER: Well I was driving along Bay Avenue, and a dog ran out in front of my car.
OFFICER: A dog ran out in front of your car.
DRIVER: I had to stop real fast, so I jammed on my brakes. And the car in back of me hit me, really hard.

C. Repeating or Questioning Listen to these short conversations between a driver and a police officer. In some sentences, the officer is repeating the information. In some sentences, the officer is questioning the information. He isn't sure that it is correct. Listen to these examples:

Example A

DRIVER: I was driving along First Street.
OFFICER: You were driving along First Street.

In Example A, the officer is repeating the information.

Example B

DRIVER: I was driving along First Street.
OFFICER: You were driving along First Street?

In Example B, the officer is questioning the information. The intonation is the same as for a question.

Circle *repeating* or *questioning*.

1. A: I was driving along First Street.
   B: You were driving along First Street.
2. A: She didn't stop at the end of the driveway.
   B: She didn't stop at the end of the driveway?
3. A: I was backing out of my driveway.
   B: You were backing out of your driveway.
4. A: I stopped at the end of my driveway.
   B: You stopped at the end of your driveway?

5. A: I didn't see him coming.
   B: You didn't see him coming?
6. A: A dog ran in front of my car.
   B: A dog ran in front of your car.
7. A: He didn't have any taillights.
   B: He didn't have any taillights?
8. A: My car has a lot of damage.
   B: Your car has a lot of damage.
9. A: I'm not hurt.
   B: You're not hurt?
10. A: I don't want to go to the hospital.
    B: You don't want to go to the hospital?

D. Past Yes/No Questions

Listen carefully to each question. Write the first two words.

1. Did he pass the red light?
2. Did she tell the truth?
3. Did you see the accident?
4. Did you talk to the police?
5. Did he hit her car?
6. Did she go to the hospital?
7. Did you have your license with you?
8. Did he stop?
9. Did you call an ambulance?
10. Did he have a lot of damage?

UNIT 15: My Neighbor

COMPREHENSION (pages 85–87)

C. Key Words Listen to the sentences and fill in the correct words.

1. The man mugged an old woman and ran away with her purse.
2. The thief beat the store owner, then stole the money.
3. The alley between the buildings is dark and dirty.
4. When I was driving, an ambulance passed me.
5. My neighborhood is noisy and busy.
6. I am upset. When I saw my friend yesterday, she acted like she didn't know me.

Story

One morning I was walking down Fourth Street. I was going to visit a friend. As I was walking past a park, two men jumped out and mugged me. They took my coat and my money. They beat me, then they left me in an alley.

A short time later, a man passed by the alley. He was from my neighborhood. I shouted, "Help me." I knew he was going to help me. He said, "I'll get the police." Then, he left. I waited, but he never came back.

A few hours later, a second man passed the alley. I called, "Please help me." I knew he was going to help me because we went to the same church. But he acted like he didn't see me. He turned and left.

It was getting late. I knew I needed help. It was almost dark when a third man passed the alley. I didn't know him. He dressed differently. He wasn't from my country. I didn't think he was going to help me. But he saw me and felt sorry for me. He stopped and called the police. He stayed with me and waited for the ambulance.

The next day, the doctor said to me, "It's a good thing that man stopped and helped you. You almost died. Who was he, a neighbor?"

I thought for a minute, then said, "Yes, he was."

E. Listen and Write the Letter Listen to these sentences. Write the letter of the correct picture.

1. He stopped and called the police.
2. We went to the same church.
3. He dressed differently.
4. Two men jumped out and mugged me.
5. The next day, the doctor talked to me.
6. They left me in an alley.
7. I was walking down Fourth Street.
8. A man from my neighborhood passed the alley.
9. He stayed with me and waited for the ambulance.
10. He acted like he didn't see me.

G. Comprehension Questions Listen and circle the correct answer.

1. Where was this man going?
2. Who mugged him?
3. When did the men mug him?
4. What did they take?
5. Where did they leave him?
6. How long was he there?
7. Who was the real neighbor?

STRUCTURE (page 88)

A. Listen and Write Listen to these sentences. Write the past tense verb you hear.

1. Two men jumped me.
2. They mugged me.
3. A man from my neighborhood passed the alley.
4. I shouted for help.
5. He turned away.
6. I needed help.
7. The third man stopped.
8. He called the police.
9. He stayed with me.
10. He waited for the ambulance.

PRONUNCIATION (page 88)

A. Same or Different You will hear two verbs. Decide if they are the same or different. Circle *same* or *different*.

1. call   called
2. jumped   jumped
3. walk   walked
4. turned   turned

5. act acted
6. help helped
7. stayed stayed
8. arrived arrived
9. ask asked
10. die died

B. *ed* Endings Listen to the pronunciation of these verbs.

/d/	/t/	/ld/
played	walked	rented
turned	missed	needed

Look at the verbs below. Listen to the pronunciation of *-ed*. Circle the pronunciation you hear.

1. waited
2. called
3. stopped
4. acted
5. stayed
6. died
7. passed
8. helped
9. shouted
10. dressed

CONVERSATIONS (pages 89–90)

Conversation 1:

DISPATCHER: Springfield Police.
MAN: My car is gone! Somebody stole my car!
DISPATCHER: Your address?
MAN: I'm at work. Wells Industries, 357 Second Street. I parked my car in the lot this morning. Now, it's not there.
DISPATCHER: We'll send someone right over.

Conversation 2:

DISPATCHER: Springfield Police.
WOMAN: Please! Hurry! There's a woman on the street, she's screaming.
DISPATCHER: Give me the address.
WOMAN: Weston Street. 32 Weston Street.
DISPATCHER: Stay on the line. Can you see her?
WOMAN: Yes. A man is pushing her into a car. She's trying to get away from him.

Conversation 3:

DISPATCHER: Springfield Police.
MAN: There's someone breaking into my neighbor's house. A man just broke the window and climbed in!
DISPATCHER: What's your address?
MAN: 126 Maple Avenue. It's the house on the left of me.
DISPATCHER: Don't hang up. I'm sending a patrol car. You can help us. Which window did he climb in? Can you see the window....

Conversation 4:

DISPATCHER: Springfield Police.
WOMAN: Something's going on in the apartment downstairs.
DISPATCHER: Where do you live?
WOMAN: 462 Salem. In the Salem Apartments. Apartment 4B.
DISPATCHER: What's happening?
WOMAN: Two men are fighting. They're real angry. They're shouting and calling each other names.
DISPATCHER: We're sending someone over immediately.

B. Same or Different Read each sentence. Then, listen to the sentence on the tape. Decide if the meaning of the two sentences is the same or different. Circle *same* or *different*.

1. My car is gone!
2. Hurry!
3. Stay on the line.
4. She's trying to get away.
5. Someone is breaking into my neighbor's house.
6. They are calling each other names.
7. There's something going on in the apartment downstairs.

C. The Robbery You are a clerk in a jewelry store. A few minutes ago a woman came into the store and asked to look at some expensive necklaces. Suddenly, she pulled out a gun, took the jewelry, and asked for the money in the cash register. Now, a police officer is asking you questions. Circle the correct answer.

1. What did she take?
2. How long was she in the store?
3. Was anyone else in the store?
4. What did she look like?
5. What was she wearing?
6. Did she have a gun?
7. What did she say?
8. Do you remember anything special about her?
9. Which way did she go when she left the store?

Ronnie plete going to Cheer me up